Everyday God:

Reflections on Liturgy and Life

by

Dr. Cecilia A. Ranger, SNJM

Everyday God: Reflections on Liturgy and Life

Title ID 8489560

For paperback and Kindle

ISBN-13: 978-171921 8580

ISBN-10: 171921 8587

Printed in the United States of America

First edition

TABLE OF CONTENTS

Dedication

I cannot prove that I was born. I have no birth certificate. But, I have documents that attest to the fact that I was baptized, received First Holy Communion, was Confirmed, pronounced First and Last Vows as a Sister of the Holy Names of Jesus and Mary. I also received diplomas from elementary school, high school, a Bachelor of Arts Program, a Master of Arts Degree, and a Doctor of Philosophy.

I did not do it alone.

I *dedicate this book* to parents, teachers, friends, professors, religious educators, clergy, bishops, Ecumenists, writers, civic leaders, administrators, political leaders, corporate sponsors, artists, and all of those who have spent their own lives empowering other people to live their lives more fully and meaningfully.

Dr. Cecilia A. Ranger, SNJM

Acknowledgements

One of our Sisters often referred to me as a "Depression Baby," primarily because I am "into" recycling paper and other material products, even the labels on soup cans, and the fact that I can put together a second-hand wardrobe for $20 that looks like "Fifth Avenue." The days since post-Depression U.S.A. have given me many decades to be immersed in Liturgy and Life, and I leave behind me a very long "trail of blessings and thank-you's-owed."

I have been blessed during my life by many people whom I have encountered in the many ministries to which I have been assigned as a Sister of the Holy Names of Jesus and Mary:

- My parents and siblings, Theodore, and Elizabeth LaVina, who birthed me (as oldest), Patrick, Lucia, Edward, Bruce, and DixieLee Elizabeth and taught us to love and care for each other, despite the fact that we seem to have been born on different planets.
- The Sisters of my SNJM Congregation all over the world, who not only blessed me with a magnificent liberal arts education but also who kept me ever aware that we need to embrace a very large world view and nourish a very deep inner world.
- All of my Interfaith sisters and brothers, of both Eastern and Western heritage, who continue to teach me that Holy Wisdom wears many multi-colored vestments while praying in lyrics that make hearts soar to the heavens while reaching out dirt-stained hands in service to humankind.

- My Catholic (Universal) Church and leaders like Pope Francis whose arms embrace the whole world as Family, living together on "Our Common Home."
- Students of every age and educational setting —high school teens, university students, adult parishioners, seminarians and clergy, novices and vowed sisters and brothers—who taught me the meaning of the Paschal Mystery with their life stories of successes and struggles.
- Blessed Survivors on the street, in shelters, in low income housing and apartments, who model for me the meaning of gratitude for every kind word, gift, action, or smile; I am often reminded that I could not survive more than two weeks on what life has to offer each of them.
- The World Around Me that I see, hear, taste, touch, smell, and love—from my little Lady Slippers (state flower of Minnesota), to the Crayfish in the creek, to the rain that soothed our faces as we walked to school, to the Milky Way that I dreamed-under, to the majestic mountains that I skied-down; the world is "charged with the grandeur of God."
- Refugees, war victims, Mother Theresa's dying loved ones, the homeless, those who have been deprived of an expansive education, the voiceless, the unemployed, those without health insurance and adequate care, the lonely and forgotten, those who are repulsed by others because of illness or disability—all who suffer because we forget to be Gospel people who are indeed "our bother's keepers."
- All the supportive people who have pushed me to finally start seeking money to publish the five books, numerous articles, and poetry that sit on my computer like lonely pieces of mosaic.

1
Preface

Theology means "the Study of God." Since the initial formation of human communities on Planet Earth, people have asked questions about the miracle of the Sun's warmth, the mystery of seeds becoming plants, the awesome phenomenon of tiny birds learning to fly, the nourishment of rains refreshing the earth—and all the wonders about the Source of all Creation. Human beings engaged in rituals that we now call liturgies to demonstrate their gratitude for the marvels of Life. Much later scholars tried to explain these truths and wonders, trying to put into contemporary language the truths about their Faith that have endured for centuries. These complexities of Theology now have names: Christology, Pneumatology, Trinity, Ecclesiology, Eucharist, Mariology, Liturgy.

Don't panic! Every one of us is a theologian. In what sense? We too "try to make relevant the enduring truths of our Faith or beliefs" for each new period of history. This book had its origins in the weekly articles I wrote for the bulletin of The Madeleine Parish in Portland, Oregon, where I attempted to uncover some of the theological thinking that rested under the liturgical readings, and to show their relevance for our day. Our too kind Bulletin Editor wrote:

EDITOR'S NOTE: On November 18, 2012, Sister Cecilia wrote in her initial Theology Corner, "Every one of us is a theologian...." With fewer missed weeks than most of us have thumbs, Sister has brought the Word of God to us with her signature style and insight, making the academic accessible to all...

Often, I have heard, "I don't get anything out of Mass (or Worship Service), so why go?" Possibly many Christians have not taken time to reflect on these truths: (1) Sunday Worship is about God, not me, about the Community offering with Jesus the Christ their Thanksgiving to God for all gifts; (2) each Liturgy "speaks" to my life here and now, so it is worth listening to and reflecting on in order to "get the message for me." That is the purpose of this book: to offer a few "triggers" gleaned from the Liturgy that might enrich our thoughts and our daily lives. Thus, *Everyday God: Reflections on Liturgy and Life.*

JANUARY

2
The Wealth of Nations Shall be Brought to You

Jesus' Welcome to All Nations

For many nations the feast of Epiphany (Manifestation) is celebrated, not the December 25 Nativity we call Christmas, as the recognition by the Gentiles of Jesus as the Newborn King of the World. The Magi saw a glorious Sign in heaven; followed the Light of their Star; presented gifts from a foreign land; and were welcomed by The Light of the World. Isaiah 60 tells his readers: "The glory of the Lord will shine on all nations, and they will walk by that Light."

But King Herod did not like the message about an Infant King. The consequences were tragic for many of God's children, brothers of the Incarnate God in a Manger—who were to lose their lives because of one man's jealousy. The Glad Tidings to Angels, Shepherds, and Wisdom Dignitaries from the East became a Sad Lament.

A TGIF World

We "look to the heavens" more than we realize, in our global TGIF (Twitter Google iPhone Facebook—courtesy of my graduate student) world of rapid satellite connectivity. We know the "Good News" of these tools for "web-ing" people in our now-small global world: Grandmothers contact grandchildren, students from Africa take online courses in Oregon, parish staff e-mail the community in minutes, all across the U.S.A. and throughout the world people hear about and respond to Hurricane Sandy and other disasters. But, as in Herod's time, we know of: teenagers who bully or demoralize peers on Facebook, hackers who cause millions of dollars' worth of damage for every nation and corporation, identity thieves who wipe out resources of innocent persons.

Gifting and Welcoming in Our Interconnected World

We also bring the Gold of kindness to e-mail and Facebook-Twitter messages, refusing to undermine persons or write negative comments on religion, politics, family, parish, school. We let the waves of our Frankincense drift beyond our small individualistic worlds, to listen to folks of other cultures, religions, political views, economic levels, ages, sexual orientations—broadening our world views to become richer, deeper, more interesting persons—"the best version of ourselves"? Could we offer the aromatic Myrrh of support, congratulations, assistance, pat on the back, iPhone call to family and colleagues? We too are Lights to the nations, using our contemporary gifts of TGIF—like the Magi, unlike Herod.

3
Wisdom Begins in Wonder

Scripture tells us there were three bearers of gifts for the Newborn King, bringing Gold, Frankincense, and Myrrh. Moved by the Wonder of a Star, they took a path that led them to Wisdom Incarnate lying in a Manger. The prologue of John's Gospel offers a precise identification of this Christ with Wisdom, describing the *Logos'* (Incarnate Word's) Christological (Anointed Messiah) role [1:3], Jesus' role as the model of human knowledge (the Holy Child who learned about life, in Bethlehem and Nazareth and Egypt) [1:9], and even as mediator of special revelation [1:14]—the three roles of the pre-existent Logos-Wisdom. Pretty complex inter-woven theology in these Gospel readings!

Currently, we can gather and offer a lot of Knowledge as gift, from: travel to new cultures, websites, books, newspapers, lectures, TV shows, radio broadcasts, listening to friends, watching parents and grandparents, listening to the questioning of children. But Wisdom is deeper than gathering Knowledge, more universal, more lasting. Wisdom demands a lot of living, leaving, listening, learning, lamenting, laughing, and loving. Confucius said long ago: "By three methods we may learn Wisdom: First, by reflection, which is noblest; Second, by imitation, which is easiest; and Third, by experience, which is the bitterest."

One of my student seminarians brought me a present, a black and white picture of an elderly man, wrinkled face artistically half-hidden in shadow. Michael said: "I knew you would like this photo, because you can see Wisdom written in the lines of his face." Maybe that is why Pope Francis has urged the elderly and the young to spend time listening and talking to each other: the Wonder behind the child's questioning leads us to risk opening doors to new Knowledge and skills, and the hard-earned Wisdom of the grandparent assures the young person that all will be well—eventually.

As we reflect on the Epiphany, and the Three Gifts of the Wise Figures from the East (some say South), we recall the ways our gifts of Gold (material resources?), Frankincense (mysteries and surprises and challenges?), and Myrrh (struggles and losses and grief?) have softened us, made us more loving, and shaped us—to become truly Wise Persons. Wisdom begins in Wonder, and Wisdom can also mend our Worlds.

4
Magi and Ecumenism

An Ecumenist since I grew up in Minnesota with an Anglican Father, a Roman Catholic Mother, and Lutherans as relatives and neighbors, the Magi have always added a certain completeness to the Christmas story. Magi (Latinized) were of the priestly class in Zoroastrianism; they paid special attention to stars and gained international reputation for astrology—a highly regarded science at that time. They were referred to as *Magoi* in Greek. Various traditions claim these Three Wise Persons were from China, Arabia, Persia, India, Western Europe (British Isles or France), Abyssinia, Ethiopia, Yemen. In the Gospel they were distinguished foreigners who responded to a call of ecumenical love. The Feast of the Three Kings (Epiphany) is celebrated by many members of both Eastern and Western Christian Traditions: Catholic, Protestant, Orthodox.

After 2000 years people and nations have yet to kneel, as they did, at the feet of Jesus, Son of God, Savior, Messiah. Deceit and cruelty of governments and individuals still exist. The greedy and technologically-equipped still uproot people from farms which they have tilled for generations, to provide water for building of dams and making money; trafficking of human beings for sex, labor, soldiering, is known across the world; selfishness, individualism, and even "righteousness" are factors in de-humanization and torture of people in every nation. Some sectors of the world look like vast cemeteries.

And yet, we witness people of every race and religion holding and healing Ebola or flu victims, even contracting the disease as a result. People respond to the food and medical needs of children; health care professionals travel the world to do surgery on deformed bodies; young people give a year or more of service as volunteer educators, coordinators of farming techniques, re-creators of entire villages that have been destroyed by natural forces. And every parish tries to provide food baskets for the hungry who live in their own villages.

Three distinguished foreigners followed a Star and brought Gifts of Gold, Frankincense, and Myrrh—symbolic of the gifts of Time, Talent, and Treasure that we share with our sisters and brothers. Despite the "Herods" of the world, we come together, recognizing that we are co-heirs, co-partners of Jesus Savior—Christians and Jews, Zoroastrians and Buddhists, Native Americans and Africans, people of every Culture and Religion, who bring our gifts to help redeem the people of the entire world.

5
O Holy Child

"Do-ing" theology as well as studying theology: take the child and his mother and flee...

A reflection on Pastoral Theology. The great Canadian Theologian, Bernard Lonergan SJ, claimed that Pastoral Theology was at the apex of theological studies. We can study and KNOW about moral, liturgical, systematic, Biblical, spiritual theologies; but Pastoral Theology challenges us to DO theology. In that sense, each of us is a pastoral theologian; we live our Faith at Eucharist or Worship and also in service to our world. Joseph and Mary KNEW about the power of the coming Messiah, were even astounded that this theological truth happened with the coming of the Incarnate Messiah into their arms. Yet, when Joseph heard the angel tell him to be a refugee, "Take the Child and His Mother and flee into Egypt," he DID it.

Safeguarding the Child

We need to safeguard the Child—in ourselves and all the world's children. Joan Chittister, in her new book, The *Art of Life*, writes: "It is the freshness of childhood that makes the mundane delightful, that allows adults to play peekaboo and patty-cake again. Without that we become creatures of argument and caution, reluctant to risk, afraid to enjoy." On the other hand, we also want to DO something about situations that deprive young people of their childhood. Joan Chittister continues: "All over the country, all over the world, children are being bought and sold, beaten and killed, abandoned and—worse, perhaps—simply ignored by the very people they depend on for food and care and love and security."

Doing Theology Where We Live

I have a friend who earned an MA in theology, but who DOES theology in concrete ways: (1) she goes to Goodwill outlet stores, fills the back of her car with jeans (pays by the pound), launders them, and takes them to Burnside, and (2) she with others started the "backpack with weekend food" project in different areas of our country so children and teens can provide food for their families. As I reflected on the marrying of theoretical theology and pastoral care, I wondered if we might consider adopting for Lent a "clean jeans" or a "backpack of food" project—during winter cold and before individual or community gardens produce vegetables to share. Perhaps we could JUST DO IT as Nike reminds us.

6
I Formed You...
a Covenant of the People
(Isaiah)

Jesus Himself was baptized, the One we claim to be Head of the whole Mystical Body, our human family. Our Baptismal Covenant is a very social reality! The Christian Community calls the baptized individual into a greater “yes” than his or her personal relationship with Father, Son, and Spirit...a mystical “belongingness” and stretching of community boundaries to include a concern for all of God’s People of every race and religion.

Pope Francis described our “Church belongingness” in this comprehensive way: “I prefer a Church which is bruised, hurting, and dirty because it has been out in the streets, rather than a Church which is unhealthy from being confined and from clinging to its own security.” Isaiah invites everybody to “come to the water” without money...without cost; to drink wine and milk; to heed God, delight in rich fare, and live. And, we are the baptized ones who make this possible.

So, what might our Baptismal Covenant ask of us now? The needs are so monumental that it is a temptation to close doors and cling to known securities. This leads me to set up a few guides which make reaching out to bruised and hurting and dirty causes possible for me—and maybe you as well.

- Match the talents God formed in me with some special community need, because trying to do everything is overwhelming.
- Select a minimum of causes to which I send money, despite the fact that I receive dozens of requests; in my case, educational deprivation (spiritual and professional), homelessness, and hunger.
- Concentrate on empowering those I "help," instead of playing the role of "great mother," gives others the chance to achieve or create for themselves.
- Realize that "more things are wrought by prayer than this world dreams of," and so embrace the entire world in prayer, especially needs of this decade: human trafficking, water as a human right and a social responsibility, unemployment, homelessness, lack of reverence for human life (wars, crises of refugees, disrespect for life from unborn to the very elderly).

Meditating on our Baptismal Covenant at the beginning of each year may be more help in giving us a sense of direction than making a list of New Year's Resolutions.

7
My Chosen One With Whom I Am Well Pleased

Every year I have tried to engage family and friends in the celebration of my Baptism: March 30, in Fergus Falls, Minnesota, on the Feast of St. Fergus, but I get "duh" responses. You see, my feast day is November 22, Feast of St. Cecilia, and my birthday March 6, formerly the feast of Perpetua and Felicity. Though I was reminded I should be "perpetually felicitous," my birthday is often during Lent (and forgotten) and my feast day is near Thanksgiving (and forgotten). But, Baptism means more to me than either of these: Jesus Himself valued it, and came to John the Baptist to seek Baptism, for "it is fitting for us to fulfill all righteousness." The Voice from Heaven said, reflecting the words in Isaiah, "This is my Beloved Son, with whom I am well pleased."

What would happen if each of us, on our Baptism Day, spent an hour in reflection: What marvelous doors have opened for me, because I have been privileged to be baptized "In the Name of the Father and of the Son and of the Holy Spirit"? Doors opened to forgiveness and healing and spiritual nourishment, to a welcoming Worship Community, to sacred commitments to marriage or ordination or religious consecration, to a ceremony of "good-bye" with relatives and friends as we return to the Creator who fashioned us as "chosen ones."

But more: it widened our worlds to embrace all Christians and Jews, those of all Spiritual Traditions, and those who are Seekers.

Baptism drew us into the *Gospel of Joy*, as Pope Francis names it, and invited us, with St. Paul, to reach out and touch others, "The love of Christ urges us on" (2 Cor 5:14). In other words, to quote Francis, "Life grows by being given away, and it weakens in isolation and comfort. Indeed, those who enjoy life most are those who leave security on the shore and become excited by the mission of communicating life to others."

If we are more inclined to read a book before the fire than go out for a brisk walk on a cold January day, we can search the web for *Evangelii Gaudium,* (*The Gospel of Joy*), or any story about Jesus' Baptism.

8
They Call It Ordinary Time

Often we've heard people sigh, "I'm bored!" They're not interested in joining the family for Monopoly; they're not interested in strolling through the Mall with friends; they could "care less" about serving sandwiches at Blanchet House or a soup kitchen. Daily life is just too ordinary.

Our daily lives are interspersed with Celebration Times: weddings, birthdays, graduations, new jobs, new friends, new driver's licenses, new clothes, new iPads and times with all of the people and events and "things" that delight us. The Catholic and Protestant Churches too highlight the year with Special Seasons: Advent, Christmas, Epiphany, Lent, Holy Thursday, Good Friday, Holy Saturday, Easter, Pentecost. But then, as is the case in our daily lives, there are periods of Ordinary Time tucked between these great Liturgical Events and Seasons. And, some people seem to "get bored" and stay away from the community's Eucharistic or Worship Celebrations and don't want to get involved with visiting the homebound.

The Biblical picture of "God resting," telling us to make room for Sabbath in our ordinary lives, could be a fine "paradigm" for Ordinary Time after Christmas and Epiphany. What if we looked on January and February, Ordinary Time before Lent, as Sabbath time? We could make a Sabbath retreat on Friday, Saturday, or Sunday afternoon or evening: walk and meditate in the park, have tea on the patio with a spiritual book, share a coffee with a homebound person, visit the Blessed Sacrament and pray the

Rosary for world leaders (many religions use beads for meditative prayer and Jewish friends use tassels). We could garden, knit, "putter" in the workshop as we reflected on a CD. We could arrange to meet with a spiritual guide or share with friends our reflections on a spiritual book.

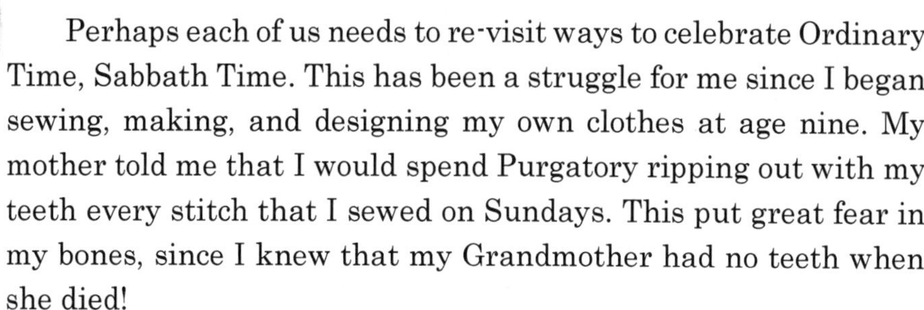

Perhaps each of us needs to re-visit ways to celebrate Ordinary Time, Sabbath Time. This has been a struggle for me since I began sewing, making, and designing my own clothes at age nine. My mother told me that I would spend Purgatory ripping out with my teeth every stitch that I sewed on Sundays. This put great fear in my bones, since I knew that my Grandmother had no teeth when she died!

The Church offers no such threat. We are instead offered an opportunity to learn to relish Ordinary Time, just as we delight in Festive Times.

9
Ordinary Time and the Spirituality of Work

Our Biblical Foundation is a Story of Workers

The Church designates, between Epiphany and Lent, "ordinary time," work time. Our Biblical roots say God created...saw it was good...blessed what was produced...and rested on the seventh day from all the work undertaken as Creator. In the Wisdom Literature (Qoheleth [Hebrew]-Ecclesiastes [Greek]) women and men were applauded for wisdom and skills at work. Centuries later, in Jesus, GOD ASSUMED THE EVERYDAY. Jesus' family and friends worked: Joseph, carpenter; Mary, homemaker; Peter and the Apostles, fishermen; later, Paul, tent-maker. Inspired by Paul's dedication, Lydia, head of her household, possibly a widow, dealt in purple (garments or cloth) and became an influential follower of Jesus.

In Catholic Tradition Work is Integral to Being Human

From Creation to Jesus' time to now, we regard work as a manifestation of the giftedness and dignity of persons. In recent times fifteen social justice encyclicals called the world to respect the rights of workers. It is interesting to read one from the web, during Lent.

- *Rerum Novarum*, Pope Leo XIII, 1891, industrial revolution, political change;

- *Quadragesimo Anno*, Pius XI, 1931, ethical challenges of workers after Great Depression;
- *Mater et Magistra*, John XXII, 1961, after WWII, cold war began, technology increased production, but poverty was world-wide;
- *Pacem in Terris*, John XXIII, 1963, cold war, collapse of Berlin Wall, Missile Crisis;
- *Gaudium et Spes*, Paul VI, 1965, Church's social teachings for a changing world;
- *Laborem Exercens*, John Paul II, 1981, dignity of human work in contemporary world;
- *Caritas in Veritate*, Benedict XVI, 2009, love is force that leads to work for justice and peace.

Workers Realize Daily New Invitations to Wholeness

Work is one expression of our spirituality. We can bring to it CREATIVITY, some new way of doing "same old"; SKILL, through education and seeking a mentor; PRIDE in being a superb mechanic, gourmet cook, teacher, lawyer, writer, retiree-volunteer, parent, employer—or entrepreneurial salesperson like Lydia. Vatican Council II reminded us: "laity are called to make of their apostolate, through the vigor of their Christian spirit, a leaven in the world." A lady checking my bag and identity, in a N.Y. library, smiled at me and said: "When ya loves Jesus, it kinda sticks out all over ya."

10
Nurturing a Culture of Call

During "ordinary time" the Sunday readings call us to beyond-the-ordinary responses to God's calls. Samuel hears the voice of God and responds, "Here I am" and "Speak, Lord, your servant is listening." Paul reminds us, "You are not your own." And the disciples who asked Jesus, "Where are you staying?" received the answer, "Come, and you will see." Initially Samuel did not recognize the interior Call as coming from God; Paul made it clear that one's body-whole self was a Temple of the Holy Spirit, God's Dwelling Place; and Jesus knew that deep down it was Himself whom the disciples were seeking. During "ordinary times" of rest, confusion about one's body, attraction to the "New," women and men continue to receive God's Call.

Even though we live in a world of noise—roaring vehicles, loud repetitive music, jet planes, and humming computers—we can cultivate a Culture of Call. First, we can listen to gifts and talents of family members, friends, students, colleagues, those who live and work by our sides, affirming, asking questions, accompanying to retreats, and generally supporting others as they discover who they are. Secondly, we can listen to them as they share interests, compassion for a particular group of people, concerns about the future of Church and World, wonders about Life. Thirdly, we can pray for them as they listen to God's Spirit helping them "match" their gifts with specific needs.

In such a Culture of Call in our homes and Churches and work settings, young and not-so-young persons will feel more secure about answering God's invitation to Come and See. Recently I spoke to a loving woman who had entered a convent, but listening more carefully to the "still small Voice" of God felt drawn to have a family. Not so recently I have listened to women and men, now parents, who had been afraid to become a Sister, Brother, Minister, or Priest, but now felt it matched better who they really are.

Together we Christians can create a listening, loving, spiritual culture which facilitates "Match-making" between inner spirit and outer needs, and moves persons to answer the Calls of God to be mother and father, priest or brother or sister or minister, missionary doctor or nurse, pro bono lawyer to poor or aging, corporate executive who shares profits with employees, low-paid director of a soup kitchen, long-distance truck driver, contemplative nun or Trappist monk.

11
The Community Celebrates Eucharist or Worship Service

Community Worship Precedes Theological Explanation

The history of Liturgy reminds us that human communities stood awestruck under the beauty of a rainbow, laughed gleefully when a new life came into the world, wept together over the Mystery of death, gathered to thank the Creator for a bountiful harvest, and worshipped the Giver of all Gifts. The truth is: we, and all human beings before us, gathered the Community for Worship before theologians began to speculate on ways to explain the meaning of God, human origins, the questions about destiny, and the theology of Eucharist or Last Supper. Liturgical Celebration and Worship by the Community have always come before intellectual analysis and explanations of religious truths.

The Playful, Prayerful Community Celebrates More Fully

The community celebrates, laughs over, and cries about Mardi Gras, a crab feed, a wine-tasting, a staff-sponsored open house in the rectory, an exchange-of-prayers Christmas tree, a Baptism or Wedding or Ordination or RCIA reception, a bereavement gathering, creation of a rose garden, raising funds for a missionary school, and even a cemetery for electronic equipment. We bring a loving, welcoming Community to each Celebration where we offer and receive together the Incarnate Son of God. Some people claim the Mass is "too scripted," "boring," and "repetitious." Yet we need "scripted words" to sing the "Star Spangled Banner" together; we drink our cup of coffee at the same "boring" hour each day, and we need to know the "repetitive" steps if we are to waltz smoothly with a partner. Ritual, liturgy, song, dance, the Eucharist--all need a pattern of words and movement if the Community is to act or Worship as one.

The Church wisely invites Christians to celebrate Mardi Gras before Ash Wednesday: Shrove Tuesday, a day of dancing, feasting, and oftentimes genuine childlike hilarity. Christians are incarnate people who recognize the joys and sorrow, gifts and burdens, blessings and deprivations of being fully embodied. They with Jesus offer to the Creator—in festive play and in celebratory Worship—all the richness of human life.

FEBRUARY

12
Presentation in the Temple

Christians have cherished the Feast of the Presentation since the fourth century. Roman Catholics, Orthodox, Anglican, Episcopal, and Lutheran communions celebrate it under the names of Presentation of Jesus in the Temple, Candlemas, Feast of the Purification of the Virgin, and The Meeting of Our Lord, God and Savior Jesus Christ. Its long history is based on Jewish law: the parents had to "buy back" their child on the 40th day after birth, by offering a sacrifice in the Temple, in Jesus' case a pair of turtledoves (pigeons). On that same day the mother was ritually purified. The words "...a light to the revelation of the Gentiles" gave rise to the custom of blessing candles on this feast. A procession took place through a darkened church while Simeon's canticle was sung. In the USA all candles to be used during the year, as well as candles of the parishioners, were blessed on this day. The next day, with crossed candles, the priest and other ministers, bless the throats of congregants; it is the Feast of St. Blaise.

Not only is the Presentation a special feast for most Christians, but it also highlights the commitment of women and men who have presented themselves to be consecrated to God by vows. In some dioceses, the Bishop celebrates in the Cathedral a Liturgy for consecrated religious women and men.

Pope John Paul II expressed the significance of this day in a 1999 homily: "The Feast of the Presentation of Jesus in the Temple creates a ... 'hinge' which separates and joins the initial phase of

His life on earth, His birth, and its fulfillment, which is His death and resurrection. Today we leave the Christmas season behind and move towards the season of Lent." He added a line which is in keeping with the Church's focus on evangelization: "Consecrated persons make a crucial contribution to the work of evangelization, bringing to it the prophetic power which comes from the radicalness of their evangelical choice."

The Feast of the Presentation is an occasion for special prayer for women and men who have made this "presentation in the Temple," and for all who are discerning whether this may be their vocation in the Church.

13
I Have Loved You With an Everlasting Love
(Jeremiah 31:3)

The World celebrates St. Valentine's Day! Religious commemorations take place among Anglicans, Lutherans, Eastern Orthodox, and Roman Catholic communities; and romantic love is celebrated in countries from China to Wales. Though many Christian martyrs bore the name Valentine, the St. Valentine honored on February 14 is Valentine of Rome, a priest martyred in 496 CE. The Liturgical celebration honors him as one who was imprisoned for performing weddings for soldiers and for ministering to Christians, persecuted for their beliefs under Roman Law. The story is told that Valentine healed the daughter of his jailer, Asterius. An embellishment adds that before his execution he wrote a farewell letter ending "Your Valentine."

The day was first associated with romantic love at the time of Chaucer, and has added more elaborate flowers, edible creations, musical cards each year. We remember the laborious hours we spent cutting construction paper and lace doilies to make sure every family member and classmate received "Your Valentine."

I have often been teased because I like to send Valentine cards, as well as Christmas gifts and yes, birthday cards (in addition to Facebook and Jacquie Lawson e-cards) that tell others why I value their presence and giftedness in my life. Perhaps everyone needs Liturgical as well as romantic festivals, especially during the "ordinary times" of our lives, to nudge us to say the loving things we have been thinking—but putting off. I recall that I wrote "love" notes to everyone I cherished, prior to cancer surgery; since then I try to let people know I care, to congratulate others, to be articulate about the lovely things I notice about them or their accomplishments.

People who experience the loss of a loved relative or friend will often say with great sadness and regret, "I wish that I would have told him or her that...." A day like St. Valentine's Day jolts us into sending flowers, selecting a delicious box of chocolates, sending a card, taking a loved one to dinner, and speaking from the heart, "I love you...Your Valentine." Let's join our Anglican, Lutheran, Orthodox sisters and brothers, and all lovers, age two to ninety-two, and say, "I love you" to significant people in our lives.

14
Super Bowl

Did you know that the shortest month of the year is one of the most important? One year I noticed Feb. 6, Pay a Compliment Day; Feb. 11, Don't Cry Over Spilt Milk; Feb. 14 Valentine's; Feb. 18, Ash Wednesday; Feb. 26, Introduce a Girl to Engineering. The list was terribly long!

But what tops all lists is SUPER BOWL. Statistics, from the past 48-plus Super Bowls, about every score, every player, every detail of the plays are available to the reader. Did you know that the Pittsburgh Steelers won six out of the eight times they have participated? And that the New England Patriots have also been finalists eight times?

It hit me. Wow, Super Bowl! What a super paradigm for our "catholic" universal Church! Millions of people are united around a Common Cause, on location, on Television, on Twitter, on every species of Social Media. People change their menu to pizza, chips and beer. All family members gather, and in the same room: father, mother, teens, young children, grandparents, cousins. Friends join in the boisterous laughter and groans as the teams vie for First Place. Careful preparations involved all kinds of professionals, travel agencies, hotels and motels, restaurants, commentators, technical experts, groundskeepers, and thousands of paid employees. And, the reason we are involved in the first place has to do with TEAMWORK on the part of the Patriots and Seahawks, and whichever team is a "winner" to us.

SUPER BOWL is one colossal happening that engages people from the Unites States and all over the world.

Always the "what if" visionary, I ask myself and us: What if our Universal (Catholic) Church took such a paradigm seriously, and applied it to our current experience?

- Common Cause: carrying the Joy of the Gospel "to the finish line."
- Inviting others to Mass, lectures, retreats, and spiritual growth opportunities, through Social Media, and many means of communication now available.
- Arranging family gatherings to celebrate in prayer grandma's 90th birthday, Cindy's First Communion, Nat's Confirmation, and the wedding Mass of Jonas and Melissa.
- Attending to careful preparation for the sacraments, the forgiving experiences we put off for years, the expressions of gratitude that we are always going to "get around to."
- Building teams wherever we work and play and pray, careful not to put forth the "my way or the highway" attitude.

As we gather with millions of others every Super Bowl Sunday, maybe we can envision this Experience of Unity as a model for healing our fractured, angry world.

15
Rainbow: Sign of God's Covenant

V-I-B-G-Y-O-R. Violet, indigo, blue, green, yellow, orange, red. The many colors making up one Rainbow. Many of us remember memorizing long lists by making a word of the first letter of each word in the body of information we were asked to learn. Before there were written Hebrew texts, our Jewish forefathers and mothers learned by rote the many Psalms they prayed in unison, because acrostic Psalms were alphabetically ordered verses with each first word commencing with a letter of the Hebrew alphabet, from 1 to 22, *aleph, beit, gimel, dalet, hei, vav*, etc. There are many examples in our life experiences of "the many different realities united to make a single one": e.g. rainbow, acrostic psalm, even the healthy human body.

Vatican Council II emphasized pluralism in unity. Each of the early Christian Communities had its own way of telling the Good News (Gospel), though we have retained only four canonical Gospels in what we refer to as the New Testament (Jewish People sometimes call it the Second Testament). That is, within the One Church there can be a pluralism of expressions: many languages at Mass instead of Latin, a variety of musical forms and instruments, adaptations for children and other age groups. Some parishioners prefer a quiet contemplative Mass or Service, others a Mass where everyone knows and participates in singing the hymns, and some people would prefer that a superbly trained choir would lift their hearts. But, all express the essence and unity of the Eucharist.

What we sometimes forget is this: every PLURALISTIC element is needed if the ONE is to become what it is meant to be. The rainbow would not be a complete rainbow if Green or Red were missing! Each of us brings our own special person to each Eucharist in order to make complete the one worshipping Community that offers all of our gifts with Christ to the Father. Though we are tempted to think "nobody cares, and I won't be missed," especially when it is wet and rainy outside, or when we have had a full week at work, plus soccer practice, plus grocery shopping, plus visiting a sick relative, etc.; yet, without each of us the community at worship is not quite complete.

One of the hymns in *Breaking Bread* attempts to put this pluralism in unity idea into song for us: "We are many, yet we are one. We are separate yet bound in God's love. And together we are all God's Hands and Feet, bringing mercy and peace to our world." I am thinking this may be worth a few moments of weekly meditation for each of us.

16
The Greatest of These is Love

The books and movies we loved as children often depicted a heart on a tree trunk with the initials of two people joined by "loves." Looks like we began nourishing in ourselves, in a way we could afford, St. Paul's universal call to Love: "There are three things that last: Faith, Hope, and Love. And, the greatest of these is Love."

This Christian Liturgical Year moves us, with the dramatic symbol of carrying ashes on our foreheads, into the Season of Lent and toward a culmination of the Paschal Mystery of Holy Week. Lent is our time to both deepen and broaden our heart's capacity for Loving God, our own true selves, the special people with whom we live and work, our brothers and sisters throughout the world, and all the "goods" with which the Creator surrounds us. It is in this sense that we intentionally leave behind our indifferences to any or all of these "goods" in order to grasp those things that facilitate our taking off any masks that hide our True Selves—where we live and love as visible reflections of the Divine.

Lent invites us to: "Bring Our True Selves to Holy Week." I like the way a colleague summed up this motto at a meeting:

> *...behind our everyday mask are things-people-ideas-needs-values to which we are indifferent. They separate us from each other, from our world and from our God. These things can be very big or very small, in the world or in our families, in the community or in our minds. During Lent, we ask the Holy Spirit to help us examine these things to*

which we might be indifferent and discern the sources of the indifference. Then during Holy Week we will begin to peel away the mask, and move beyond indifference... And at Easter we dispose of the mask and reveal our true selves...

As all of us gather for the Great Triduum (Holy Thursday, Good Friday, and Holy Saturday) to prepare for the Resurrection Celebration (Easter) of the One Whom we worship as True God and True Man, we recognize that we have made a sincere effort to become true reflections of the Creator who shaped each of us so uniquely and lovingly.

Happy Valentine's Day!

17
Why Bother to Care?

Sometimes we simply want to "give up" on someone. My sister with poor health has ignored all of us who beg her to quit smoking. My friends and I have tried many times to dissuade loved ones from taking numerous prescription drugs. Women religious have tried for decades to explain to authorities that they need to be at the sides of God's People when and where the people live and work, if they are to serve them. I have had students say to me, "I think you spent more time editing my paper than I spent writing it. Why do you care?" At times, each of us may wonder, after years of trying, "Why bother to care?"

Pope Francis has offered as one of his Lenten messages an invitation that we shift our consciousness away from "apathy" or "indifference" or what I am calling a why-bother-to-care attitude—to be a "caring" person. His analysis applies this to three levels: the interpersonal level (which separates us from the other), the cultural level (which leads us to a lack of judgment of values and global uniformity, and a general absence of meaning in life), and what the Pope calls the metaphysical level (which leads us to become indifferent towards God and all God has created). We become caught in what he calls a "globalization of indifference," of "not caring."

If I am tempted to "quit caring" I take out a message from Father Walter Burghardt, SJ, as my "mantra." It applies to other areas of life, as well as to the Church—and helps me, and I hope you, look at the goodness in each person and situation, as well as that which troubles us. It goes like this:

In the course of a half century I have seen more Christian corruption than you have read of.

I have tasted it.

I have been reasonably corrupt myself.

And yet I love this Church, this living, pulsing, sinning people of God with a crucifying passion.

Why?

For all the Christian hate, I experience here a community of love.

For all the institutional idiocy, I find here a tradition of reason.

For all the individual repression, I breathe here an air of freedom.

For all the fear of sex, I discover here the redemption of my body.

In an age so inhuman, I touch here tears of compassion.

In a world so grim and humorless, I share here rich joy and earthy laughter.

In the midst of death, I hear here an incomparable stress on life.

For all the apparent absence of God, I sense here the real presence of Christ.

18
"Wise Guy": Immense is the Wisdom of the Lord
(Sirach 15)

My Father called me "Wise Guy"; my Mother teased me for "Putting Mind over Matter." I wonder if that's the impetus that led me to work toward a doctorate in Hebrew Wisdom Literature (i.e. Sirach-Ecclesiasticus, Qoheleth-Ecclesiastes, Job, Proverbs, Song of Songs).

I cherish theologian Elizabeth A. Johnson CSJ's words about Wisdom Literature:

> *The rediscovery of the Wisdom Tradition is widening the theological playing field for discourse about Christ... unlike the Historical and Prophetic books, the Wisdom Tradition is interested not only in God's mighty deeds in history but in everyday life with the give and take of its relationships...salvation history is not the only way, indeed for some not even the primary way, that religious experience occurs. People connect with the Holy Mystery that surrounds their lives as they actually live in the world...*

Let's listen carefully and non-judgmentally to people when they share with us that stones, trees, a puppy, a rushing ocean, fish in a clear lake, a smile of an elderly person, a young woman on her wedding day, a man or woman at ordination or profession of vows speak to them of the Mystery of God. Jesus told us in parables about God's breaking into our everyday lives when he spoke of wheat and weeds, lilies of the field, preciousness of the child he held on His knee. The Wisdom Teachers and the Tradition which they left to Jesus had spoken about these things centuries earlier.

God chided Job for being a "wise guy," asking: "Can you raise your voice among clouds? Can you send forth lightning on its way? Who tilts the water jars of heaven so that the dust of earth is fused into a mass and the clods made solid?" After being reminded of the ways that "God's Hand touches all of reality," Job admits: "I know that you can do all things, and that no purpose of yours can be hindered. I have dealt with great things that I do not understand, things too wonderful for me... I had heard of You by word of mouth; now my eye has seen You."

The Biblical Wisdom Writers remind us to see God in all that exists!

19
Listen…to Be Transformed

LISTEN…TO MY BELOVED SON

God did not respond very favorably to Peter's suggestion that he, James, and John might build three shrines, for Jesus, Moses, and Elijah, on that Mount of Transformation. From the cloud God offered an alternative to Peter: "Listen…to My Beloved Son." Listening to God's Son Jesus is the way we hear the daily insistent messages about God's preferences for our actions that can lead to our own transformation—maybe without experiencing the glory of having shrines set up for us, except in our own hearts.

Ascetical Theology gets our attention during Lent: spiritual disciplines, meditative listening, almsgiving, Stations of the Cross, generous services to those in need, praying about and following the ways that Jesus responded to His temptations. As Paul invites us in Philippians 3: "Join with others in being imitators of me (i.e., Paul, who said, 'I live, not I, but Christ lives in me'), and observe those who thus conduct themselves according to the model you have in us."

FEED THE RIGHT WOLF

A native American Grandfather told this "listening" story to his Granddaughter:

> *I feel as if I have two wolves fighting in my heart.*
>
> *One is vengeful, angry, and violent. The other is loving, kind, compassionate.*
>
> *The girl asked, "Grandfather, which wolf will win the fight in your heart?"*
>
> *He answered, "The one I decide to feed."*

The Season of Lent gives us 40 days to step back from many of the wolves that devour our time, energy, leisure and humor, family gatherings, regular attendance at Eucharist or daily Awareness Examen or prayer, commitments to others, and just simple graciousness and spreading joy to those we meet each day. Listening to our thoughts, imaginations, memories, inner dialogues, "urgings," body signals—as well as to the ways other people, nature, and everything in the world around us—provide us with "discernment data" to find out what God prefers for us.

With the Native American Grandfather we need to decide which wolf we will listen to and feed.

20
One Does Not Live by Bread Alone

Food Wonderful Food

Funny topic for Lent? You can hear the words of the waifs in "*Oliver*." "Food wonderful food." God gave us a land flowing with milk and honey, pizza and beer, and fruits and vegetables from local gardens and now those from Chile and Mexico and many places in our world. And, the freedom to celebrate these good things which the Loving Creator has given us! Still, the hungry live in Oregon, as well as Africa, Asia, South America, and Haiti. Recently I visited an E.M.O. (Ecumenical Ministries of Oregon) food bank at a Church, which distributes donated food weekly, and reaches out to 10,400 families a year.

Spiritual Freedom and Food

Catholics before 1962 were called by Protestant friends "the ones who couldn't eat meat on Friday." The challenge of Vatican Council II stretched our spiritual world views to realize that most people in the world could afford neither meat nor fish—any day. The Church challenged us to a mature level of spiritual freedom: to make choices about Lenten sacrifices, to offer with Christ who lived the Paschal mystery of suffering, dying, and rising something of a real cost to us personally—with the motives of spiritual emptying, *metanoia*, freedom of spirit, and care for others. More than "giving up," we learned to "stretch out and give" to others:

food backpacks, window cleaning for the elderly, doctor trips for the infirm and veterans.

Non-Food Fasting

The "fasting" can be non-food, a "mind-fasting," for us of any age and health condition. We can make daily efforts to "fast" from retaliatory remarks, put-downs, negative thinking, too much talk about health, concentrating our thoughts and feelings on psychological or physical hurts, mean-spiritedness, resistance to hearing healthy criticism, and those thoughts and words that keep us from being FREE IN THE SUFFERING, DYING, AND RISEN Lord. My father had a roll-down desk with tiny shelves—a great tool for "filing" away un-resolved issues that needed to be taken to prayer at a later time, not "stuffed" or "ignored" or "repressed."

Whether the sacrifice is food, wonderful food, a costly offering unique to oneself, or a refraining from negativity, we can slip it in the offering basket, where "The priest shall take the basket from our hands and set it in front of the altar of the Lord."

21
Living Eucharist

At the end of every Mass we hear the deacon say words like: "Go, the Mass is ended. Go forth to live what you have experienced." Having received the Body and Blood of Jesus the Christ, we spread out, as a community of believers, to make a difference in our world, each sharing our unique talents with our families, friends and colleagues.

The Greek word for Eucharist is "thanksgiving." We can imagine Jesus with the Apostles at that meal where He made the offering of Himself in bread and wine. And we recall too his action of foot-washing, with the invitation to serve as He had served. The Jesus who said "Do This in Remembrance of Me" also told His followers: "You call me 'teacher' and 'master,' and rightly so, for indeed I am. If I, therefore the master and teacher, have washed your feet, you ought to wash one another's feet. I have given you a model to follow, so that as I have done for you, you should also do."

Thanksgiving for giftedness, gratitude for blessings changes the way we encounter every event! A few years ago, someone gave me a small journal called "The Gratitude Book." In it, the journalist writes five things each day for which she or he is grateful. Amazing how it opens one's eyes to the beauties of people, distasteful tasks, and all our daily world of burdens, surprises, challenges, blessings. Soon I had a difficult time limiting the writing of blessings for each day to five.

Interesting that Jesus left us this "memorial meal" to remind us weekly, or daily, to be people of Thanksgiving. The many negative criticisms of leaders can sometimes weigh us down; and yet, if we begin to search for occasions when we could say "thank you" to those who serve us, the culture around us could be more hopeful, helpful, harmonious, and happy.

We can also engage each other in small Living Eucharist groups, blessed occasions to learn more about each other and also to be strengthened and invigorated to try to live more wholeheartedly, with the support of loving and prayerful companions, that invitation to "Go, the Mass is ended. Live the Gospel with your life."

MARCH

22
Stretch Our Gifts and Our Minds During Lent

This is what Yahweh asks of you: to act justly, to love tenderly, and to walk humbly with your God. (Micah 6:8)

We can remember the "give up for Lent" days: no meat, no chocolate, no movies, no parties. These were deprivations which promoted self-discipline. Yet, they tended to keep the focus on oneself, and the great transformations that take place when one is deeply aligned with the Paschal Mystery of Jesus the Christ were not always uppermost in our minds. We were downright hungry to take in that Hershey bar, but not thirsty for the reaching out that calls on us to stretch our talents and resources for the sake of the hungry. By that I mean: What if we exchanged a "give up" notion of Lent for a "share giftedness" one? What if we "fasted" from attitudes that kept us and our worlds small instead of stretching them to include everyone who is hungry, hurting, or helpless?

It would truly be a win-win Lent! "A Fast That Transforms," moves us in that direction. We can reflect on our best gifts and skills: Listening to people? Teaching Scripture? Leading prayer groups? Visiting the sick? Fixing someone's computer? Digging up a vegetable bed for someone with a handicap? Volunteering at a shelter or dining hall? Reading to a homebound person? As we share these gifts and skills we notice that they are refined still further—transformed.

Often, I used to meditate on the value to myself and others of "mind-fasting," and tried to make it real in my life—especially in Lent. What if we "fasted" from the negative thoughts that creep into our minds when someone insults us? What if we "fasted" from the comments we would like to make when we are angry at a situation? What if we "fasted" from putting ourselves down, in thought or word? What if we "mind-fasted" from all of those reflections that keep us from becoming a just, loving, tender, humble, grace-filled person?

Stretching our gifts, instead of giving up something outside ourselves, and fasting from thoughts that keep our worlds too small, transform the world outside us—and ourselves as well.

23
Baptism: New Awakening of Soul

March 30 is my Baptismal day: Feast of St. Fergus, and I was baptized in Fergus Falls, Minnesota on a wintry day. Fortunate for me, there is a record at Our Lady of Victory Church, because I was born at home and no birth certificate exists. I had to be born, if I was Baptized! When the pastor who baptized me died, they found in his breviary the letter I had written him, thanking him for that precious day and informing him that I had entered the convent. That is the day I celebrate: the day of my Baptism.

The Catholic Church welcomes new catechumens and candidates into our Faith Communities throughout the world, "In the Name of the Father, and of the Son, and of the Holy Spirit." And we renew our own Baptismal commitments and promise to offer loving support and challenge to these new members of the Communion of Saints. Our souls are re-awakened, as we recognize God's new life birthed in each of them.

For the Christian of today, as in the first centuries, Baptism is still the entrance to all the Sacraments, the gate to Christian life, and therefore to eternal life, which is the ultimate eschatological consequence of our living out faithfully this Call to share in the Divine Nature. Descent into the water washes away our old mortality (inclination to choose sin); ascent from the water is the passage from death to new life. Theology today looks on Baptism as a Paschal Sacrament, the sacrament of a person's

"Passover" from death to life, to Resurrection and New Life in Christ.

But Baptism is not a "zap" experience. Baptism imposes daily and life-long obligations in keeping with the new spiritual nature of the baptized: to be a responsible and responsive Christian, to turn one's back on destructive habits, to commit oneself to the following of Christ crucified and risen—simply, to try to follow God's personal and communal invitations without reserve.

During the Paschal Triduum we journey with the newly baptized and the candidates as they advance toward full participation in the Eucharist at the Easter Vigil. We also re-awaken in our souls the awesome miracle of bearing within our very beings the Presence of Father, Son, and Spirit.

24
The Master Has Need of It

THE MULTITUDE PRAISED GOD WITH JOY

At first things looked good to the disciples as they entered Jerusalem. The people were putting down their coats, waving palm branches, and saying: "Blessed is the King who comes in the Name of the Lord. Peace in heaven and glory in the highest" (Lk 19). Or: "Hosannah! Blessed is he who comes in the Name of the Lord" (Mt). We have had those times when we received A's in our studies, applause for our good work, special awards in music or sports or academics or for another talent, and knew the joy and honor of being "center stage" for a while. The experiences made the thermometer of our self-concept zoom up quite a few notches. All the people who selected us for the honor felt proud and grateful as well.

PALM SUNDAY IS ALSO CALLED THE PASSION OF THE LORD

As he drew near Jerusalem and wept over it, Jesus reminded the disciples, "For the days are coming upon you when your enemies will raise a palisade against you...They will smash you to the ground..." How often the very people who applauded Jesus, and us, at a later time will take the opposite position of criticism, meanness, accusations, jealousies, even betrayal. Praying with Jesus as we read the Passion, about His betrayals, makes our own easier to grasp—betrayals by disciples, friends, spouses, children, employers, colleagues, and parishioners. Betrayal by one whom we love and trust may create a deeper wound than any other sin.

The Master Has Need of Us

Imagine Jesus having to borrow a donkey to take that ride into Jerusalem, because, he told the disciples, "The Master has need of it." Let's remember this scene: Jesus needing people and even other beings like the little donkey. We Catholic Christians and others are in fact needed by the Master to carry the burdens of the wounded veteran, the poor orphan, the elderly widower, the handicapped athlete, the wealthy deaf or crippled person, those in authority.

It seems a little strange to say to ourselves, "The Master has need of me." But the Palm Sunday reading of the Passion brings this reality to life for us. We can experience times of affirmation and later betrayal, sometimes brought about by the same persons.

25
We are Easter People

AND ALLELUIA IS OUR SONG!

Attributed to St. Augustine (354-430 CE), ancient Roman Theologian, these words lift our hearts on Easter Sunday, and will hum in our hearts all year long. "We are Easter People, and Alleluia is our song." They echo similar thoughts of St. Irenaeus of Lyon (130-202 CE), first great Western ecclesiastical writer and theologian, who emphasized unity of Old and New Testaments, Christ's human and divine natures, and the value of Tradition. He reflected "The glory of God is a human being fully alive..." A holy card that I cherished showed a little boy running breathlessly, with these words written beneath the picture: "I have come that they may have LIFE and have it abundantly." The Faith of over a billion Catholics young and old, across continents, north and south, sing a new Alleluia of Hope for the Holiness of all members of Our Church.

CIRCLE THE WORLD WITH ALLELUIA-SONG

Recently a famous experiment in meditation-prayer was recorded. A group of people formed a circle around the city of Washington, D.C. and meditated continually for a period of time. Gathered in this circle of love and kindness Washington changed! The statistics for that period in the city showed a remarkable and unprecedented decrease in violence and crime. So what if the billion plus Catholics, Protestants, and Jews, as well as those embracing other Traditions, made a circle of Alleluia song and carried ourselves as Easter People wherever we go? We could circle every block, our homes, our workplaces, and the places we go for leisure, with the spirit of which St Augustine spoke. Because we are Easter People who know how to celebrate: the Paschal Mystery, all Sunday and Sabbath and Friday celebrations, pancake breakfasts, potlucks at Living Eucharist sessions, picnics in the park, and any party for which we can think of a plausible excuse! At this time in the history of almost every nation in the world we need a large circle of Easter People. We have no idea of the effect we actually have on one another!

26
One Sows and Another Reaps
(John 4:37)

A few years ago, I was "fighting battles" with authorities, as a leader trying to create feasible retirement plans for the Sisters, who have an un-funded retirement. Since 1859 the Sisters were offered by the laity the use of a convent and car, discounts on doctor and dental and hospital bills, turkeys and hams at holidays, $25-$100 monthly stipends, tuition and music lesson money, and gifts for the "common pot" which Sisters miraculously stretched to meet personal and ministerial needs—and looked forward to having many younger Sisters fill their shoes in classrooms and other venues when they retired. To my Assistant I wondered aloud, "In what generation will these efforts to provide for the retirement of elderly Sisters become realities?" In her kind way, she responded, "If it's of the Spirit, it doesn't matter when or who gets the credit."

Most of us have worked very hard trying to help our children develop their gifts, doing our best to create new systems in the workplace, offering fund-raising plans for new facilities or parish ministerial programs. Often, we have not been able to see our hopes and dreams and efforts realized. We sowed; another reaped the results.

The Samaritan woman was given marvelous gifts: Jesus, a Jewish man, spoke to her; He actually asked to drink out of her clay vessel; He spoke her own Truth to her; He promised her Living Water; He told her that He was the Messiah, the Anointed, the

One to Come. She responded by being one of His first apostles, leaving her water jar and proclaiming to the villagers, “Come. see a man who told me everything I have done. Could he possibly be the Messiah?” She sowed the seed!

The Samaritans began to believe in Jesus, not because of the woman who had testified. Villagers concluded: “We no longer believe because of your word; for we have heard for ourselves, and we know that this is truly the Savior of the world.” How often children, students, colleagues, friends, authorities who have been recipients of our plans, sacrifices, even our love come back to tell us,

> “I discovered...”,
> “I created...”,
> “I accomplished...”,
> “I was rewarded for...”,
> “I succeeded at....”

There seems to be little recognition that all of us stand on the shoulders of others.

One sows. Another reaps.

27
Why This Waste of Perfumed Oil?

Family members and friends have sometimes said of us who made vows as Sisters, Brothers, or Priests: "But you could have ...." (the rest of the sentence often has to do with using our "smarts" and other talents to make money). Or, at times they shake their heads and sigh, "What a waste!"

Their comments make me think of Mark's Palm Sunday Gospel: "Why has there been this waste of perfumed oil?" The answer is: because she who poured that oil on Jesus' head "got it right." Jesus the Messiah, the Anointed One of God, is worth the waste of perfumed oil.

He Who gave His all, is worth "wasting" one's life, to follow in His footsteps. I carry the memory of a man who left his motel room to come to question me. He shared, "I was in my motel room, planning to commit suicide. But, I decided to come to see you first. I was thinking that you tossed your whole life in for the sake of Something, so there must be Somebody 'upstairs.' I want to know why you did this." We talked for hours. The suicide did not happen. The "waste" was worth it.

Each of us pours oil on the wounds of others, often without realizing the long-term effects of our "wasting" time, giving without receiving, being some place or speaking some words because of God's inner urges. It's the phone call we make, the time we spend over a cup of coffee listening to heartaches, the sitting at a bedside of the sick, the visits to the homebound, the support of a teenager trying to work through the complex issues with which she or he is confronted in today's world, or the time we spend in Adoration before the Blessed Sacrament interceding for a world that is scarred and confused and fighting meaningless wars.

Maybe we accomplish more for those we love, for our friends, for our church, for our nation, for our world—by pouring oil on wounds and wasting time in what we call a Ministry of Presence, than we would by making millions of dollars for a corporation. These "wasted endeavors" create meaningful lives for us, whether we are 15, 45, 65, or 85!

28
Life-Giving Power of Friendship

Jesus' friend died, and Jesus wept—then healed His friend. And Lazarus' sister, Martha, leader of an early Church community, proclaimed as did Peter, also a leader in the early Church: "I believe that you are the Christ, the Son of God, the One Who has come into the world."

In *The Joy of the Gospel* the section entitled "*Yes to the New Relationships Brought by Christ*" Pope Francis reflects, "The Gospel tells us constantly to run the risk of a face-to-face encounter with others, with their physical presence which challenges us, with their pain and their pleas, with their joy which infects us in our close and continuous interaction." Sometimes we become alarmed when we notice a table of six or eight people at a restaurant, each talking on a cell phone; and we question whether they know skills of socialization which assist them in the workplace, at parties, and in all their interactions with people. We even feel a certain sadness, wondering whether they know how to engage in face-to-face encounters, where friends can affirm their gifts and challenge their actions and attitudes—gifts which help us identify who we are.

Successful citizens have often been urged by friends to take risks, to use their God-given talents for the good of humankind. Performers like Peter, Paul, and Mary worked together for decades—claiming it was possible because they were good friends. Friends can indeed help us climb ladders of success.

Friends can also help us heal when we fall off the ladders. Or, when we sustain a loss of a loved one, health, employment, our home, financial stability, or any hurt which causes our hearts to grieve. A friend may not understand fully the depth of our sorrow, but he or she knows us well enough to listen and to empathize with us on a deep level.

We notice throughout the Gospels that Jesus shared many special moments of His life with friends: the Baptism, the wedding at Cana, the Last Supper, the Agony in the Garden, the Transfiguration, the Journey to Emmaus, and even the moments after the Resurrection with Mary Magdalene. To be deeply loved by one's friend opens the heart to live genuinely the Greatest Commandment: "You shall love the Lord with your whole heart and soul and mind, and your neighbor as yourself." In the face-to-face loving of friends, we ourselves become healed and whole.

29
Nothing in Common With the Samaritans?

At a Jungian meeting, when one of the women discovered I was a "nun," she walked out of the room. (As time went on we found we had more in common than she anticipated, and we became friends.) A few decades ago, Catholics were not to mingle with members of other religions, even Christians, and their restrictions were similar to ours. Nothing in common? Sometimes we pass panhandlers, looking the other way, because we do not know what to say or what to give these people who do not live as we do. Discovering what human qualities we share in common with those who seem strangely different from ourselves challenges us to "walk in the other's moccasins," as our Native American sisters and brothers suggest—especially if we are to view the world as others experience it.

Jews and Samaritans had shared a common history until the defeat of Israel's Northern Kingdom in the 700s BCE, but they were distanced from each other at the time of Jesus. Jesus greeted her and invited the Samaritan woman into a deeper and richer relationship as their conversation progressed. He even made a request that you and I may have considered beneath our dignity: He asked her to do something for Him, to give Him some water from the well. In exchange He offered her Living Water. He spoke to a woman, and a Samaritan at that; He would drink out of an "impure" cup; He would associate with a sinner who was ostracized by other women who came to that well. How amazing: all the "rules" were seemingly set aside, and forgiveness and discipleship happened—she became a messenger to the entire village and a key figure in the Gospel.

In the Lenten process of inviting Catechumens and Candidates into the parish community, we are saying to these "newbies" -- "All are welcome." The "process" Jesus presented us in His encounter with the Samaritan woman is the perfect initiation to draw people to a Faith Community:

- He greeted the woman reverently.
- He asked something of her, setting aside what was "proper."
- He pursued the conversation to a comfort level, in which she revealed herself and He revealed His identity as the Living Water and the Messiah.
- He saw her as a special "human face" and not just any Samaritan.
- Jesus respected her just as she was.
- Moved by the encounter, she became a missionary, admitting to all people in the village that Jesus told her everything about herself, asking: "Is He not the Messiah, the anointed one, the Savior of Humankind"?
- As a result of their meeting, many persons believed, not on the strength of her testimony, for they had to walk through the door she had opened and find out for themselves who Jesus was.

Perhaps, the next time we judge we may not have anything in common with someone, we might review the story of Jesus and His encounter with the Samaritan woman at Jacob's Well.

30
Many People Do Not Like Change

You may have heard often, "I hate to have things changed." It is often true: people would rather keep or live the known than risk the unknown, even if change is more life-giving for their spiritual, mental, or physical health. Think of the abused person who stays in a relationship, even though it is dangerous for her or him. Or the employee who hates the job, and yet stays with it instead of seeking one that is a better fit for the talents and interests that one has identified. Or, changes in neighborhood, leaders, liturgical worship, vocations of our children. Change is not a friend to all persons.

Jesus' disciples were amazed at His Transfiguration. He did not appear to be the familiar Jesus they knew! Quite often when we decide to change, people are uncomfortable with the "new me," because it suggests they need to interact with us in a changed way. They would rather have us remain as we were, even if we had been alcoholics, persons who offered a negative analysis of every religious or political or domestic event, or relatives who have decided to be unforgiving and not to speak to certain family members. Change is indeed difficult or puzzling for many: the changed person as well as the observer of the changed or converted friend or relative or colleague.

The Feast of the Transfiguration suggests that we could be called to transformation. We begin to ask such questions as:

- What vision for my future surfaces when I pray and reflect on who I am and who I want to be?

- In what activities do I glimpse transfiguring visions for our society today?

I pass these questions on to all of us because they invite us to personal meditation, evaluation of our lives, and *metanoia* (conversion or CHANGE), on the one hand. And then to leaving behind our Indifference to people and earth and church so we are free to DREAM about the future of our needy world and those who are suffering.

Transfiguration invites us to change, to pray together the Paschal Mystery: the suffering, death, and resurrection of the One who stood on that mountain and amazed His friends, Peter, James, and John. And, us too.

31
Why Do We Need Saints?

SAINT PATRICK, MODEL THEOLOGIAN (387-460)

If the job of the theologian is to make enduring truths of Christianity or any Tradition meaningful for each new period of history, Saint Patrick-Padraig fit the bill in the fifth century. This apostle of Ireland used symbols (shamrock) from Irish pagan beliefs in his teachings about Christian beliefs and sacraments; and he is said to have devised the beautiful Celtic Cross-pattee. Though Patrick's father was Calphurnius-Calpornius, a deacon from an elite Roman family, his mother Conchessa, a relative of St. Martin of Tours, and his grandfather Pontius-Potitus a member of the clergy, Patrick was not "well-schooled" in religion. After he was taken from Roman Britain to be slave and herdsman at age 16, his master Milchu was a high priest of Druidism. Patrick escaped after six years, studied in Auxerre, France, and became a Catholic priest under the guidance of St. Germain, missionary. Tradition records that Pope St. Celestine I consecrated Patrick as Bishop of the Irish. Patrick died in 460-461 in Saul, Ireland, and was buried in Ulster. Catholic, Orthodox, and Episcopalian Traditions celebrate the feast of St. Patrick. Many of us have enjoyed Thomas Cahill's book, *How the Irish Saved Civilization*, because of Ireland's isolation and escape from the plundering of literary and cultural resources when mainland Europe was sacked by marauders.

Communion of Saints

One of the Catholic doctrines I most value is that of The Communion of Saints: the belief that all of us, living as well as those who went before us, are connected in a spiritual solidarity, an organic unity called the Mystical Body or the Body of Christ. If my Faith wavers at times, I think of great theologians like Patrick, Rahner, Haring, Johnson, and other brilliant, faithful theologians I have known or prayed to—other members of the Communion of Saints. We request of each other, "Will you pray for me?" and trust that those prayers will be heard by the Christ who is Head of the Body. Finally, speaking of the Irish, the practice of "kything" is one in which persons like us send spiritual energy and prayers to another for healing, discernment, or any need; even if the recipient is unaware, the Irish believe that those prayers will be effective. So do I.

APRIL

32
Palm Sunday with Our Ecumenical Sisters and Brothers

One of my most memorable Palm Sunday celebrations took place in the parking lot of a Portland Catholic Church, where Catholics, Presbyterians, Lutherans, and other Traditions met to hear the Word of God and the Sermon and to bless the Palms. After this Liturgy of the Word, the Christians from the respective congregations processed joyfully, palms in hand, to their own churches to continue their Palm Sunday liturgies. I stood there deeply touched at the experience of unity that we were experiencing. At the same time, I prayed that we truly might know our Ecumenical sisters and brothers, work side by side for God's People who need us, and perhaps one day celebrate Eucharist together at one Table of the Lord.

After such experiences I often return to the Vatican II Decree on Ecumenism (*Unitatis Redintegration*) for motivation to make every effort to advance the Ecumenical Movement as one way of bringing together people who wish to work tirelessly for peace and justice. The Decree speaks lovingly of this grace: "In recent times, God has begun to bestow more generously upon divided Christians remorse over their divisions and longing for unity. Everywhere, large numbers have felt the impulse of this grace, and among the members of the separated Christian communities there increases from day to day a movement, fostered by the grace of the Holy Spirit, for the restoration of unity among all Christians."

Do we ever wonder what the world would be like if every Christian (and Jew, Muslim, Hindu, and all who reverence The Holy One) might stand elbow to elbow to free women and men from human trafficking, protest the destruction of mountains and farms and rivers by those who use those resources to their financial benefit and deprive generations of their natural beauty, or kill each other because they judge that their creeds and values are to be imposed on others? Much of my life I have had the privilege of teaching in ecumenical circles: theology to ministers, prayer and spirituality to laity, world religions to people of all ages and traditions. These rich sources of wisdom, commitment, generosity, and sanctity not only expand our hearts and minds—the experiences of listening and joining hands also facilitate the deepening of our own Faith and Commitment to the Triune God!

33
God's Grandeur in Nature

The World is charged with the grandeur of God.
It will flame out, like shining from shook foil...
Nature is never spent; There lives the dearest freshness
deep down things...Because the Holy Ghost over the bent
World broods with warm breast and with ah! bright wings.

So wrote Jesuit Gerard Manley Hopkins, whom we name "spiritual theologian," expressing his Faith-reflections in poetry. In early morning the birds and squirrels remind us that "Morning has broken," and we are gifted with another day of LIFE. As we drive to work we are astounded that the rhythm of nature has come full circle to unveil the bright yellow forsythia, the explosion of pink camellias, the smiling purple pansies, the bursting pink blossoms of the flowering plum trees. It's hard to keep our eyes on the road; and our hearts and minds struggle not to become lost in the Mystery of God's Creation that "charges" the world around us with "freshness"—once again.

Glory be to God as Ultimate Beauty
Glory be to God for dappled things—
For skies of couple-colour as a brinded cow...
He Fathers-forth whose beauty is past change: Praise Him.

From Psalmists to Matthew's Gospel we are reminded that the lilies of the field do not work or spin but "Solomon in all his splendor was not clothed like these." Spring offers us a new pallette on which we can paint insights about God the Creator. It is true that Catholic Christians make a theological distinction: We do not equate God with the forces and laws of nature (*Pantheism,* which holds that the Divine Being is synonymous with the universe), saying that we can worship that redwood tree as God. But we can take a position called *Panentheism*, which posits that the Divine Being, God the Creator, Eternal God interpenetrates every part of nature and timelessly extends beyond it; you have read of many of the saints who tell us to "see God in all things." Therefore, for many of us, Spring is restorative: it allows us to go to work early, drive or walk a little slower, look out the window at the daffodils, and say, "the world is indeed charged with the grandeur of God."

34
Holy Name of Jesus

The Holy Name of Jesus refers to the theological and devotional use of the Name of Jesus. The Name "Jesus" was common among Israelites at the time of Jesus' birth, and it means "Yahweh saves." In ancient times, a Name expressed the person's place in the universe, and could express a person's mission or even his or her destiny.

Matthew's Gospel refers to Jesus as "the One who saves the people from sin." In fact, Matthew provides the beginnings of a Christology of the Name of Jesus: it affirms Jesus as savior, and it also emphasizes that the Name came about as a heavenly command. Luke 1:31 claims that an angel told Mary to Name her child Jesus, and Matthew 1:21 says that an angel tells Joseph at the time of his first dream, "You shall call His Name Jesus, for He will save His people from their sins." John too has Jesus say, "If you ask the Father anything in my Name He will give it to you." Mark speaks of demons being driven out in the Name of Jesus, and Luke's Acts invoke the Holy Name when baptisms take place or when miracles are performed. Paul's Romans reiterates the saving nature of the Holy Name, stating that to those who call on the Name of the Lord" will be saved. Philippians asks for a response, "In the Name of Jesus every knee should bow, of those that are in heaven, on earth, and under the earth."

The Church has responded to these invitations in the Gospels and Epistles in many ways. Christian prayers end with, "Through Our Lord Jesus Christ." Because Christians identify symbols as having intrinsic Divine power, they hold that invoking the Holy Name of Jesus can bring about peace or provide protection by repelling evil.

Devotions to the Holy Name of Jesus are common in both Eastern and Western Christianity, since the early days of Christianity where it was placed on altars and vestments. Medieval devotions were promoted by Anselm of Canterbury in the 12th century, encouraged by Bernard of Clairvaux, and official recognition given to the Holy Name by Pope Gregory X, at the Council of Lyons in 1274. By the 15th century Bernadine of Siena promoted the devotion, and even John Calvin and Martin Luther encouraged confidence in and meditation on the Holy Name.

A number of religious congregations are dedicated to the Holy Name of Jesus, including the Society of Jesus and my own Sisters of the Holy Names of Jesus and Mary. From the Eastern Churches, many people throughout the world use the Jesus Prayer as a daily mantra. Invoking the Holy Name of Jesus has brought peace and healing to people for 2,000 years.

35
Jesus in the Mundane

Reading the Gospel of Luke, we might conclude, "Jesus tried everything, to convince the Apostles that He was The Messiah, the Anointed One, the Son of Man as well as the Son of God." The Disciples on the road to Emmaus did finally recognize Him in the breaking of the bread. Of other Disciples Jesus asked them to look at His feet and hands, to touch him, to remember that ghosts do not have flesh and bone. Finally, at the end of John's Gospel, He asked the very mundane question, "Do you have anything here to eat?" And He took the baked fish. Only then did Jesus open their minds to understand the Scriptures, after which He sent them on a mission to go out as witnesses about all they had seen, heard, and experienced.

The great German theologian, Karl Rahner, consultant at Vatican Council II, offered the profound statement: "In today's world we Christians must be mystics or nothing." He described "mystics" as those who see God in all things, even the ordinary: all that we see and hear and experience. In the Northwest, mysticism can be a daily as well as a seasonal reality. We see blossoms develop into plums or apples or cherries, leaves turn all shades of green and yellow and red and brown; we smile at the antics of squirrels; we feel mist and showers and downpours on our bodies. Moreover, we are surrounded by mountains, rivers, the ocean, fields of black soil or green grass. And, the most dramatic reflection of God and God's Presence are the people we meet each day—the

People of God that together make up the living, breathing, Body of Christ.

Truly Jesus does reveal Himself in the mundane, all the words and acts and encounters we experience each day—the breaking of bread, the touching and hugging, the one-to-one conversations and the family and community gatherings. Our invitation: to live all of these experiences with awareness that each moment of our lives is touched by God, that all we say and do can be a witness to the mysticism that ignites the hearts of others to also "See God in all things." When people experience that "un-definable something," that Presence, they want to know and experience more. What better method of evangelization?

36
No Needy Person Among Them...

Luke's Acts of the Apostles, chapter 4, gives us a portrait of the newly-formed Christian community: they shared all their possessions in common, so that there was no needy person among them. The concern of their hearts was to provide for the common good.

We may have seen the movie, *Pay It Forward*, in which a young boy took this goal as a class project and then passed it on as a life project. Abigail, 10, formed CareGirlz, an ensemble of girls 6 to 13, to present Broadway hits to residents in assisted-care centers. The project of Ryan, 6, to build a well in Africa, led to Ryan's Well Foundation, providing clean water and sanitation to 714,000 people. Dylan, 9, co-founded Lil' MDGs, to leverage the power of digital media to engage children in UN millennium development goals. Jackson, 11, and Tristan, 9, started the non-profit Backpacks for New Beginnings for kids who could not afford school supplies. And Condon, a high school senior, transports vets to their appointments. Somewhere in their DNA or their developing young hearts is a concern for the common good of others in our world.

So, from where do comments like these arise?

"My needs are...", "Not in my backyard...", "My way or the highway...", "Let those who follow us be concerned about the environment; I want to have what I need, and I want now..."

Many registered voters do not believe their votes can make a difference, claiming, "The Democrats and the Republicans do not care about the common good of us citizens; they only want to be re-elected or to have their own way." The Sects in Islam (especially Sunni, Shia), continue to kill each other instead of uniting to live what the Qur'an teaches. Maybe we need to remember: "When the good of everyone is protected, so is mine."

Why not, during this time between Easter and Pentecost, pray together in Faith-Sharing groups, Centering Prayer Meetings, Tuesday Adoration, Daily and Weekend Eucharistic Liturgies, and personal prayer and meditation, that our hearts may experience a "new Pentecost fire" that inflames people at work, in our families, and among our friends, to absorb into our hearts and our daily activities the concerns for the common good of all—so there is no needy person among us?

37
We Too are Doubting Thomases

It takes an egg to make hotcakes! You can have flour, powdered milk, water, a can of baking powder—but the batter needs an egg. When our family was traveling to California from Washington in a camper, stopping in a rather forlorn area, the kids were hungry. Mama, never a "Doubting Thomas" like the rest of us, knew God would provide the egg. And so it was, right there in the field alongside the camper—probably a large duck egg. But the hotcakes were delicious!

How often in our lives have we doubted that God would be present to resolve issues that seemed far beyond our own coping abilities or resources? Though we smile at Thomas' words, "I will not believe unless..." we know in our hearts that we have "been there." We also look back and remember the times we took a wrong exit from the freeway because we were distracted, only to find out later that there had been an accident which could have injured our children. Jesus does not exactly say to us, "Put your finger into the holes where the nails had been and believe"; but our gifts of hindsight unfold the number of times that God has been "present and in charge" of even the smallest details of our lives.

Maybe many of us find it difficult to believe and to hope as we look at our world, even in the miraculous Eastertide Season. It is hard to believe in people when they steal water from the poor in order to earn money through manufacturing beverages the poor could never afford. Hard to believe in civil authorities who protect their own pocketbooks and protest a living wage for others. Hard to believe in religious authorities who forget that spiritual and hunger needs do not restrict themselves to a 9 to 5 schedule. Hard to hear those who say to us, "Well, let the next generations worry about those things—not my problem now."

Nevertheless, God does ask us to "look at where the wounds are" and to believe that, together with God's gracious mercy and love, we do have the personal and communal resources to be healers. We live as Alleluia People: People of Faith, and People of Hope—in God and in each other!

38
Choose Life

Ezekiel opens the mouth of the Lord so hearers can grasp the message that gives Life: "I will put My Spirit in you that you may live...." The Christian theologian, Jurgen Moltmann, wrote an entire book called *The Spirit of Life*, where he describes the Holy Spirit as the "well of life" or "a living vigour." He sees the Holy Spirit as totally engaged with the world, giving it vitality for Life. Another theologian, Dorothee Solle, has written a book entitled *Choosing Life* and she picks up on the Moses theme: "Choosing life in the face of death means chiming in with the great 'Yes' to life...." The "Yes" which is meant in the emphatic, biblical sense, a "Yes" without any conditions.

The paradoxical relationship of Suffering and Death and Life are lived out in Love by Jesus in the Paschal Mystery, celebrated each year during Lent and the Easter and Pentecost Seasons. That is what is behind the Lenten theme, "A Fast (Suffering, Death to Self) That Transforms (Gives New Life)." The Gospel story of Lazarus is a paradigm of this Gospel of Life, for Jesus says to the wonderment of all, "This illness is not to end in death, but for the glory of God.... (and later in the Gospel) I am the resurrection and the life; whoever believes in me, even if he dies, will live, and everyone who lives and believes in me will never die."

In our time AIDS has left African orphans—children who watched their parents die, and who are now being housed, fed, educated, and nurtured by SNJM sisters and other missionaries who dedicate their lives to struggle beside these children to transform their lives and thus bring Life to others. Parishioners have supported my "passionate" efforts to raise funds to assist in this mission for God's children. A Fast That Transforms is also brought to Life in dedicated efforts to feed the homeless at St. Francis and Blanchet House, to educate children in Haiti, to bring joy to the homebound and ill, to gather prayer groups or adore before the Blessed Sacrament, gathering the needs of all who are hurting and who can find a "welcome place" in our hearts. "I will put my Spirit in you that you (and others) may live."

39
Religious Affections in the Spiritual Life

FEELINGS DIRECT US GODWARD

You can probably hear Barbra Streisand and Julio Iglesias singing "Feelings" when I land on this topic in spiritual theology. Or you still hear teacher or parent say, "Do it anyway; I don't care how you feel." Thumb through Scripture again: Cain was jealous of Abel; Sarah was skeptical of the visitors' message; Ruth was attached affectively to Naomi; Jonathan loved David as his own soul; the Magi were in awe before the Child Jesus; Herod was furious at being tricked; Jesus grieved at the death of Lazarus and He cherished John; and Psalms express rage, joy, thanksgiving, and every human feeling. The early theologian Origen taught that feelings make such a difference in the spiritual life that passions and emotions can cloud freedom, and the spirit other than the Holy Spirit moves the decisions (e.g. to strike or shoot or say hateful words). Theologian Jonathan Edwards went so far as to say, "True religion, in great part, consists in holy affections." That is, religious affection is the ability to be touched by and to respond to Someone (God) or Something (of God).

FEELINGS GUIDE OUR LIFE CHOICES

Jesuit founder, St. Ignatius Loyola, recognized the importance of religious affections (feelings) in guiding Christians in their spiritual lives. His teaching about Consolation and Desolation in discernment is more relevant now than ever, in a complex world of numerous moral, spiritual, financial, familial, employment, and other decisions facing us every day. By Consolation as a religious affection we mean: (a) feelings, usually of peace, that draw us toward God (despite their sometimes feeling "negative," like remorse or sadness); (b) feelings come from the Holy Spirit, moving us in the direction of God, goodness, common good; (c) feelings have positive consequences (drawing us toward service, deeper prayer life, loving thoughts, better use of God-given talents). Desolation moves us away from God: (a) with feelings of discouragement, unhappiness, laziness; (b) feelings come from a cause not of the Holy Spirit; and (c) the results lead to actions that are not of God. The spiritual feelings in our hearts are good thermometers of our spiritual lives and the God-direction to which they are leading us.

40
Read Literal Wording or Spiritual Message?

WHAT'S REVELATIONS DOING IN THE BIBLE?

The Four Gospels and Luke's Acts of the Apostles are primarily realistic narrative. Epistles are usually expository and hortatory prose, guides to the new Christians. But Revelations tells of extraordinary visions and prophesies; it is apocalyptic literature. You have seen full page ads about the coming end of the world, with literal quotes from Revelations. But apocalyptic literature is "code" literature. For example, "Babylon" is often read as a symbol of political power, luxury, decadence of Rome; but other symbols also represent greed and oppression. Nevertheless, Revelations is worth a read; the Church uses it in the Mass and the Divine Office. Be consoled by such readings:

"I, John, saw a new heaven and a new earth...I also saw the holy city, a new Jerusalem, coming down out of heaven from God, prepared as a bride adorned for her husband. I heard a loud voice from the throne saying, 'Behold, God's dwelling is with the human race. He will dwell with them and they will be His People and God Himself will always be with them as their God. He will wipe every tear from their eyes...Behold, I make all things new.'"

METAPHORICAL WRITING IN SACRED SCRIPTURE

The Bible consists of theological truth ("language of love"), not literal or scientific truth. The story of the 5,000 is different in John and Mark, because they were making a theological truth relevant for their respective communities. Matthew, Mark, Luke, John, Paul carried to different communities the Enduring Truths of the Faith that we pray in The Apostle's Creed. Consider the Catholic ("universal") Church Pope Francis now shepherds: the variety of cultures, languages, rituals, leadership. Look at the Church Archbishop Sample now shepherds from the Washington to the California borders--larger than his "fold" in Milwaukee. If you or I wrote a Gospel for our geographic area or community, we'd express the Enduring Truths of our Catholic Christian Faith in metaphors unique to our experiences—hopefully in images that would touch the hearts and minds of other parishioners.

How important it is to look beyond literal words (in the Bible and in Life) and to read the underlying spiritual message—as Jesus did!

41
So, What's a Charism?

WHY CAN'T WE "HAVE THEM ALL"?

When we do theological reflection on 1 Corinthians 12, we notice key truths about Charisms: (1) they are God's special gifts, spiritual as well as "skill set" gifts; (2) given to benefit the Community, not ourselves; and (3) each of us has limited gifts—we do not get them all! Reflecting on the legacy and Charisms of Pope Benedict XVI is illustrative: (1) he was a brilliant theologian who said, "The world of reason and the world of faith—the world of secular rationality and the world of religious belief—need one another and should not be afraid to enter into a profound and ongoing dialogue for the good of civilization"; and (2) he loved the Christ whom he served with what theologian Walter Burghart, SJ, would call a "crucifying passion." When scholar Benedict tried to be fair and quote a diversity of positions—this led to major difficulties for some Muslims who did not view this scholarly methodology as just. And he surprised the world by choosing to pray for the Church and do scholarly theological work instead of continuing in the public office of Pope, with the physical and social energy that it takes to serve a world becoming smaller and yet more "global" every year. Benedict was given certain Charisms, to build up the Church; but he was not given all of the Charisms that billions of Catholics might have wanted Jesus to give him.

How Do I Identify and Use My Charisms?

We might say that we are in the "same boat" as this successor of Peter the Fisherman. Each of us has been given unique Charisms for building up Community. Sometimes we envy others' gifts, and overlook possibilities for using the ones we have. Yet each has charism(s): listener to others' stories, grounds keeper, community organizer, computer specialist, Minister of prayer, skillful soccer player or outstanding player of another sport, administrator, researcher, therapist for addicts, musician, lawyer, doctor, or one who suffers and unites it with the sufferings of Jesus the Christ. Our list is much longer than St. Paul's! Friends, family members, spiritual directors help us identify our Charisms. And cries of the hurting People of God call them forth!

MAY

42
Mother

...There is no man so great, nor none sunk so low, but once he lay a helpless, innocent babe in a woman's arms and was dependent on her love and care for his existence.

It is woman who rocks the cradle of the world and holds the first affections of humankind.

She possesses a power beyond that of a king on his throne. (Michel Hale)

When we listen to "sharings" of people in Faith groups, party gatherings, or even simple story-telling sessions, the introductory clause we hear most often is "My Mother used to say..." Mothers taught us poetry, lines from Scripture, quotes from great literature, moral theology, psychology of the suffering, enough sociology to understand those who hurt us, values like justice and compassion, home-decorating, "making-do," and budget-balancing when we ran out of money. Simply recalling these lessons reminds us of the difference a Mother makes in the entirety of one's life!

Some theologians who write Mariological studies tell us that Jesus learned many of His Ministerial sensitivities from His Mother, Mary. Though Sacred Scripture reminds us that He was the son of Joseph the carpenter, we are also told that Jesus lived in a little village and seemed to have spent much time in the company of His Mother and other mothers until He was about twelve years old. He watched her, and probably the other women of the village of Nazareth, as they received guests with warmth and grace, healed wounds, taught children to read Torah, respected the Law and Authority, listened with compassion to others' pains and sorrows, held children, provided for widows, participated in Feasts, and prayed daily to the Master of the Universe. Later, at the Wedding Feast of Cana, her power of compassion is still evident; she noticed the dilemma of villagers, perhaps with limited resources, and said simply to the stewards: "Do whatever He tells you."

Our Siblings, Teachers, Bosses, Friends, and other people we have met during our lives certainly had a role in helping us make the choices which shaped our lives. But the person who seems to have had the most lasting influence on us, to this day, is the woman we call Mother. We honor and thank our Mothers and Mother Figures. We carry with us their lessons—every day of our lives!

43
A Love Like No Other

Mother's Day! We are reminded in 1 Jn 4:7-10 that God sent His Son that we might have Life in Him; and Jn 15:9-17 reflects that there is no greater love than this, to lay down one's Life for another. Each morning, when I thank God for another day of Life, I think of a tiny five-foot-tall, blue-eyed, dark-haired Irish lady who actually believed in fairies and leprechauns, and sang long sad ballads as she rocked her children to sleep, after she doused them in holy water—the one who gave life to a 10 pound baby girl, and taught me to speak so I could "beg for the moon to play with," before I was one year old. I recall too her standing over me day and night, to nurse me through pneumonia twice when I was a child. Our Mothers give us life. Our Mothers pour out the energies of their lives for us. The love of our Mothers is a love like no other!

Since ancient times Greeks knew how precious mothers were, and dedicated their Spring festival to Rhea, Mother of many deities; and the Romans made offerings to Cybele, their great Mother of gods. Later, Christians celebrated a festival for mothers on the fourth Sunday of Lent, in honor of Mary, Mother of Jesus. In England, this was expanded to all mothers and called Mothering Sunday. The United States caught up later, about 150 years ago, with Mother's Day. It started when Anna Jarvis, an Appalachian homemaker, organized a day to raise awareness of the poor health conditions in her area, asking all mothers to be advocates for this cause.

After Anna's death, her daughter is believed to have promoted her mother's efforts, quoting her as saying: "I hope and pray that someone, sometime, will found a memorial Mother's Day. There are many days for men, but none for mothers." She claimed that her mother's favorite flower was the carnation; the House of Representatives adopted a resolution that all officials of the federal government would wear white carnations on Mothers' Day. In 1914, Woodrow Wilson signed a bill recognizing Mother's Day as a national holiday.

The second Sunday of May has become the most popular day of the year to dine out, and telephone lines record the highest annual traffic. So, on this particular day, carnations to all of our Mothers!

44
No "Ordinary" Mother

We may have memories of processing into Church singing "Tis the Month of Our Mother...," wearing a dress shirt, or a white dress and carrying a lily wrapped in an enormous white bow. Mary had to be significant! (Mary is also significant in other Christian churches and in Islam.) Then there was the crowning of Mary as Queen of the May, the Living Rosary, and the many Churches and Statues bearing her name.

In fact, so important is the Blessed Mother in the Catholic Church that Vatican Council II featured her in chapter 8, Our Lady, in the *Dogmatic Constitution on the Church.* The opening summarizes:

> *The Virgin Mary, who at the message of the angel received the Word of God in her heart and in her body and brought forth Life to the world, is acknowledged and honored as truly the Mother of God and of the Redeemer. Redeemed, in a more exalted fashion, by reason of the merits of her Son and united to him by a close and indissoluble tie, she is endowed with the high office and dignity of being the Mother of the Son of God, and therefore she is also the beloved daughter of the Father and the temple of the Holy Spirit.*

The Theology of Mariology would say that this describes her identity "in a nutshell."

But to God's "ordinary" people she has many roles, as Mother, Sign of True Hope, Comfort to a Pilgrim People, Solace to Suffering Humanity. For centuries, while monks and nuns prayed the psalms and read the Scriptures, those who did not have that privilege prayed the Rosary, reflecting on the Mysteries of the Life of Mary with Her Son. Families gathered after dinner to pray those Mysteries, sometimes squirming and reluctantly kneeling during five super-long decades. When a child was ill, a job lost, a shack in New Orleans burnt, a grandparent nearing death, Catholics appealed to Mary as Mediator with Her Son to heal their wounds or respond to their needs.

Though some people mistakenly accuse Catholics of "worshipping" Mary, many who embrace a spiritual life claim that this human Woman, "blessed among women," is a unique and necessary presence for all believers. Perhaps "tis the month" to pray that she may be the Mother who unites all of us as one family.

45
Forgive Mother for Not Being Perfect

My Mother loved to share a story of her first born, when I was 2 years old. A "bum" came to the door; she only had home-made bread with butter or bacon drippings to give him. Unhappy with that meager offering, he socked her, knocking her out. She woke up with me standing over her and sopping her head with a wet washcloth, murmuring, "Poor Mommy." Almost polar opposites as we were, we always let each other be the person God created each of us to be. That is why I am puzzled when I hear people tell me that they are not speaking to their mothers, and sometimes about "horror" stories of decades-old hatred toward the women who gave them life. I wonder what the expectation or image might be of a "perfect Mother" that she simply could not be!

Mothers' Day could be forgiveness day, an appropriate choice for the call to forgive one's mother for not being the person that I wish her to be, or to have been, for me. One of my Masters' Students wrote her Thesis on Forgiveness. Life had not treated Judy kindly: she grew up with adopted siblings who were not kind and gentle to her; her son was imprisoned because he was in the company of a group who harmed another individual; she had to divorce her first spouse and raise her children alone. She became a Ministry Student and was ordained; her congregation loved her and she did much good; sadly she was killed instantly by a truck when a group of ministers at a convention crossed a street. Despite the fact that "life had not been fair" to her, her Thesis was this: To

Fail to Forgive Hurts the One Who Does Not Forgive More Than It Does the "Wronged Person."

Samuel Taylor Coleridge wrote: "The love of a mother is the veil of a softer light between the heart and the Heavenly Father." Though the language is not inclusive, I admit, it may be an invitation to each of us to search for the softer light in our Mothers. And to forgive the dark moments we may have experienced.

46
Ascension Thursday: Change of State Rather than Location

When I was a literal-minded child, I worried there wouldn't be room in heaven for every human being. Of course, I had no idea that Jesus' Ascension was about a change of state, not location. Later, when I taught at seminaries, Ascension Thursday was a much-anticipated date: the last day of classes and beginning of a welcome summer break!

Narrated in Luke 24:50-53 and Acts 1:1-11, and implied elsewhere in the NT, this feast was important to the early Church as a "marker." It marked the end of the 40-day period during which the Risen Jesus appeared to disciples (Acts 1:3). It also marked the point just after which the Holy Spirit would be poured out in power on the early Church (John 7:39; Acts 2:33-34). Thirdly, it marked the beginning of the Glorified Jesus' sitting at the right hand of the Father (Romans 8:34; Ephesians 1:20-23; Colossians 3:1; Acts 1:11).

After this 40-day period, there would be no more bodily resurrection appearances of Jesus—despite declarations by Christians from the 1st to the 21st centuries. The Church would classify such experiences as visions, dreams, or something other than Jesus' bodily appearances to believers, even appearances later on to Paul—important because the Christian Church throughout history would need to contend with innumerable reports of appearances of the Risen Jesus, as well as declarations about new revelations! So, the Ascension marks both the end of Jesus' resurrection appearances and the end of the Church's receiving his authoritative teachings.

Secondly, the disciples must have been puzzled and frightened when Jesus told them, "It is to your advantage that I go away" (John 16:7). But the arrival of the Holy Spirit (Luke 24:49; Acts 1:8) meant that the work of Jesus would continue and thrive, as the Body of Christ, in His Church and the Eucharist.

Finally, the Ascension of the Lord means for us that he has preceded us and created a pathway for us to dwell eternally in the Kingdom of God with our Glorified Jesus. Though we will not ascend to heaven in the same manner, we too will be transformed. Human nature will be exalted.

Ascension Thursday does have something to do with my early image of Human Nature being transformed, to the extent that all human beings can now be with God eternally. Ascension Thursday gives us the opportunity to realize that Resurrection, the Coming of the Holy Spirit, and Eternal Life are not just childhood dreams!

47
Why Are You Looking at the Sky?

The Gospel of Luke and the Acts of the Apostles make up one epic story told in two acts. The Ascension of Jesus is the hinge for the two-volume work. The climax of the story of Jesus and the key to understanding the beginnings of the Church lie in the Ascension story—the significance of which is often overlooked by most of us Christians. Yet, we pray in every one of our Creeds: "On the third day, He rose again; he ascended into heaven (40 days after Easter), and is seated at the right hand of the Father..."

Our preconceptions of heaven can get in the way of the understanding of Heaven that was confessed by the early Church. In the early Church the emphasis was not so much on a Place, but on being in God's immediate Presence. Acts 1:9 speaks of a cloud that took Him out of sight. In Scripture a cloud represents the *shekinah* glory of God, the sign of God's Presence (ex 33:7-11; Mark 9:7) So, our thinking needs to make a shift from spatial terms to relational terms. That is, in biblical cosmology heaven and earth are not two locations but instead two dimensions of God's creation in all that is good.

So we can speak of a "new physics" of the Ascension—seeing heaven as a dimension that can touch our present experience rather than a place far away. This contact is made possible by the Incarnation, Resurrection, and Ascension of Jesus. In a nutshell, the Word-Made-Flesh shares in our humanity in order that we can be raised to the heights of divine glory.

It is in the Spirit (who comes at Pentecost 50 days after Easter) that TIME is collapsed, and we can presently possess eternal life, though we await the fullness of Presence. In the Spirit, SPACE is collapsed, so God is present everywhere, though we wait to see God face-to-face. In the Spirit MATTER is also collapsed, as the Risen Christ is experienced now in the Sacraments, although we await final Union with Jesus Who Ascended to be at the right of the Father. So, because of the Ascension, Jesus is absent—yet present!

The question then, as we look up into the sky, is not "Where is Jesus"? But instead, "Where are we in relation here and now with the Ascended Jesus"?

48
Spirit Alive and Well

The Pentecost story tells us that the Spirit came, and inflamed the hearts and minds and voices of people from many different cultures. *Ruah*? Spirit? Breath? Wind? *Pneuma*? Indwelling of the Holy Spirit? No matter what the seemingly elusive name, the Spirit that Jesus sent at Pentecost is alive and well!

In Each Person

We seldom grasp theological truths unless we ourselves experience them. Recall times you were setting table and you "sensed" you had to get out to the yard where the kids were playing. Or, the day you were "prompted" to take another route to work and missed a 20-car pile-up. Again, the moment you were "inspired" to keep silent instead of responding with a hurtful remark to your spouse or child or colleague. And after school, when you were "moved to" turn in the other direction instead of bullying or texting something harmful to another student. Wow, all day long that Spirit is working for us. As we develop a discerning heart we become more aware of that Spirit within us, moving us to awarenesses, life-giving actions, use of the gifts-charisms the Creator gave each of us. 1Corinthians 12 speaks of those unique gifts—for building up the Body of Christ.

In the World

When we were young we created bookmarks, each symbolizing a Fruit of the Spirit. Galatians 5 names those Fruits of the Spirit: love, joy, peace, patience, kindness, generosity, faithfulness, gentleness, self-control. Listening to the Holy Spirit, acting in harmony with the "still small voice within us," and "pooling" our gifts with those of others in the Body of Christ make a terrific difference in our now globally-conscious, texting world. The Fruits of the Spirit take on flesh and become visible in us, our family members, friends, and people in our larger world. So, in this time after Pentecost, let's daily recognize in the people around us the love, joy, peace, patience, kindness, generosity, faithfulness, gentleness, or self-control that each person demonstrates—and acknowledge those gifts verbally.

What a blessing it would be for this time after Pentecost if each of us could have an Emmaus (Luke 24) experience every day: "Were not our hearts burning within us?"

49
Different Workings but the Same God

Remember when students in elementary and high school created Pentecost bookmarks symbolizing the gifts of the Holy Spirit? The Catechism aligns each of these gifts with a virtue; thus, the gift of Wisdom, the virtue of charity; Understanding and Knowledge, faith; Counsel, prudence; Fortitude, courage; Fear of the Lord, hope; Reverence, justice. As one theologian explained, "What gifts do over and above the theological virtues (and I would add the cardinal virtues) is dispose the person to the special promptings of the Holy Spirit to actively exercise a life of virtue."

Perhaps the Holy Spirit endows each person with an extra dosage of one of the gifts; for we witness "different workings" in the people we know, "though there is but one God" as St. Paul reminds the Corinthians. We do look to some friends to model for us the gift of Wisdom, some for inspiration to live Justice, others for wise Counsel or Spiritual Guidance. Sometimes I wonder what would happen to the world if each person could identify one outstanding gift and live it to the max!

The dramatic appearance of the Holy Spirit upon the early Christians was an unforgettable experience—for them and for us. And, "each one heard the message spoken in one's own language." It would seem to me that truth is both "good news" and "bad news." One hears with the language of the heart, so one's own language is understood more deeply and even effectively; that's the good news. It takes less effort to hear one's own language, but this can generate a limited world view if that's all we hear; that's the bad news. A teenager who listens to or texts only those in one's age group misses a wide range of Knowledge, Understanding and Wisdom—products of living by other age groups. An older person who does not listen with Reverence to the experiences, opinions, and dreams of young people "freezes" her or his own future. I listened to a dialogue between a woman of 30 and the other 95; both told me that they "had their minds blown open." A larger world view, in one listening session!

There is but One Spirit, and together we make up the one Body of Christ—by sharing the Gifts of that One Spirit.

50
Discernment: Responding from Our Deep "Yes"

Discernment in Real Life

Decisions! Serious as well as daily ones. Shall I go back to school and change professions, before I too am laid off? Would marrying this person help both of us become our best selves? Could I, as a surgeon-dentist, possibly serve for a month in Mississippi? As my energies decline and I may not be able to live alone, shall I consider moving to a retirement center? I will graduate in June; shall I go to college or work a year first? I am at a turning point in my life; how can I determine where I am and where to go? Discernment deals with the Mystery of God in our everyday lives.

Foundations of Discernment

Remember our Christmas gift: In the parish we were given a wonderful CD, "*Becoming the Best Version of Yourself*"? God cares and provides graces and insights we need to become our best person in:

SCRIPTURES: Recall when a Sunday Gospel-Homily moved us to change something about our lives. Or an insight from a Lectio Divina reading.

TRADITION: Cherish norms that guide us to the Sacraments, to ways to live fully seasons of Advent or Lent, to standards of behavior that foster integrity and freedom of conscience.

FAITH COMMUNITY: When we don't want to become our "best version," we think of our Living Eucharist community or friends or family who faithfully "keep on moving" in the direction of God's Mystery and call.

PRAYER: God dwells within us, has a "dream" for us, and "nudges" us toward that which is most integrating for us personally and best serves the common good.

READING GOD'S NUDGES

Elizabeth Liebert SNJM, in *The Way of Discernment*, has discernment helps for reading these nudges of God. One is meditation on our hearts' desires: Sit quietly in God's Presence and ask, "What do I want, right this minute?" Jot answers in a journal. Select the most important. Again, sit quietly before God and ask, "What is underneath this desire? What desire is even more basic than this one?" When you come to your deepest desire, honor it as central to who you are. As you discern issues that are before you, let this be KEY to God's direction for you, given the special kind of person that each of us was created to become.

51
Call to Diaconate in the Catholic Church

In the Old Testament, widows and children were vulnerable if a husband died; remember the story of Ruth and Naomi where a male relative became responsible for their care. In Acts 6 (see also 1 Timothy 3), the Hellenistic Christians complained against the Hebrews because widows were being neglected. The Twelve responded by calling forth and laying hands on Deacons (though not yet called that) to serve: Stephen, Philip, Prochorus, Nicanor, Timon, Parmenas, Nicholas.

The Tradition among the Fathers (Irenaeus, Ignatius, Clement of Rome, Eusebius) and the early Councils also referred to Deacons; the duty of serving at tables may have passed into the privilege of serving at the altar, for Deacons became the natural intermediates between the celebrant and the people, as well as the Bishops' deputies in secular matters, especially in relief of the poor, instruction of catechumens and preparation of the altar services. Acts 8 speaks of the Deacon Philip administering Baptism. As time went on duties of Deacons included: stewardship of Church funds, welcoming the poor and aged, directing congregations during services, reading the Gospel, administering the chalice and sacred host to communicants, baptizing. Though Pope Gregory forbade Deacons from chanting the Psalms, some of the most beautiful chants in the Church's Liturgy are confided to the Deacon: the Exultet on Holy Saturday, for example. In later times, the Diaconate was regarded as a stage of preparation for the priesthood; hence, there is not the same stress on precise duties. Currently we recognize both transitional Deacons who will become ordained as priests and also permanent Deacons.

Paul's letters (58 CE to Romans 16 mentions Phoebe as Deacon of the church; as well as Mary, Tryphaena, Typhosa, Persis, Euodia, Snytyche) and early Christian writers (Clement of Alexandria, Origen) refer to the role of Deaconesses; early Fathers (Epiphanius, Basil of Caesarea, John Chrysostom, Gregory of Nyssa) accepted the ministry of female Deacons, as did the Didascalia. Macrina, eldest sister of Basil and Gregory of Nyssa, was a Deacon and founder of a monastic community. Deaconesses were mentioned in a controversial passage of the Council of Nicea (325), clearly at the Council of Chalcedon (451) where women could not be ordained until the age of 40, with the rite for Deaconesses found in the 5th century Apostolic Constitutions and the Barberini Codex of 780. Olympius was a Deaconess at the time of John Chrysostom in the 5th Century, and continuing liturgical and pastoral roles seemed to have been provided by Constantine Porphyrogenitus' 10th Century manual of ceremonies. Deaconesses served women: instructing catechumens, assisting with baptisms, caring for physical, emotional, spiritual needs; though they were responsible for the women's choir, and some believe they were presiders of the Eucharist, though this practice was seen as invalid. By the 9th and 10th centuries only nuns were ordained as female Deacons; by the 12th and 13th century, Deaconesses had disappeared in European Christian Churches; there is substantial evidence of their existence throughout the history of Eastern Churches; and the Deaconess movement was revived in mid 19th century in Protestant churches. The question has surfaced again for the Roman Catholic Church in the 21st Century.

Vatican Council II called us to recall that we are all called to holiness and service, to take seriously our roles as the priesthood of the faithful and as prophetic voices in our church. Though ordination has formalized our roles as servants of God, most of us Servants in the Church are not called to ordination. Yet, we are all called to Holiness.

JUNE

52
In Praise of Fathers

God gave us many Fathers: Himself, birth fathers, step fathers, guardians, priests, theologians, spiritual fathers, teachers, and the many men who inspired and challenged us to become the persons we were created to be. We worship God the Father, along with Jesus and the Spirit. We admire, emulate, walk-in-the-footsteps-of, and are held-in-the-arms-of the fathers who nurtured us. God created the Cosmos and expected us to exercise reverent stewardship of all created beings, and fathers have borne much of this responsibility since the beginning of unwritten history of humankind.

Each year I value my own Father more than last year. Actually, most children find that their fathers become wiser every year after they themselves come of age. Though my father (Theodore, "God-bearer") had to stop his formal education after the 10th grade, as did most men of the "Depression Era" in the U.S.A., he read widely and was more politically savvy than I. He never directly contradicted my positions, but told a story or presented concrete evidence—the point of which led to the exact opposite conclusion that I had posited. Believing that girls should learn skills to make them survive independently and boys should learn cooking and other household skills, he taught me to fix cars, repair electrical wiring, pour cement, build scaffolding, paint, and survive in a tough city when I was alone. His advice was: "Walk like a bat out of hell." And my brother became head cook for 2,000 men on a Navy ship. When I visited home, he had a little gift in the dresser drawer, and smiled when I approached to thank him. Probably too sensitive for his own good, he was often taken advantage of, by relatives and clients. But, he had learned to develop both sides of his brain: the artistic and loving, and also the pragmatic and intellectual. Besides, he always loved working with me, because I could guess what he wanted when he called for a "whatchamacallit."

What a blessing we have, to set aside a day to honor God Our Father, and all the "fathers" who have nourished our gifts and challenged us to stretch beyond what we thought were our limits, and to "reach out and touch" so many people because of this. Fathers really do steward reverently God's Cosmos and all created beings—especially us.

53
Five Minute Walk with God

PUT OUT INTO THE DEEP DAILY

"Put out into deep water and lower your nets for a catch." Luke's Gospel invites us into deep waters to catch something valuable, especially at the end of a day when we have skimmed the surface of a million tasks. Awareness Examen or Consciousness Examen is a spiritual practice of pausing at the end of the day for five minutes, to "walk prayerfully through the day again," holding God's hand in our imaginations. How did I greet my spouse when I was still half-asleep? What answer did I give to the questioner who walked into my office? What about my yelling at the person who passed me on the freeway? Did I pause before I grabbed the phone so that I would answer it graciously? Did I give others in my family time to review their day while I listened attentively? Did I acknowledge the services and gifts of others? As my niece used to say, "Aunt Cece, that was a 'yuk' thing I did, or that gave me a 'yum' feeling." These "Yuks" and "Yums" happen in our hearts and spirits as we pause with God for five minutes, asking ourselves, "How was God present during each event or encounter today?" If the feeling at the pit of our stomachs or the center of our hearts was "Yuk," chances are we were not following the "nudges" of God. If the feeling was "Yum," one of harmony or peace, it was a "God thing."

THE SPIRIT IS ON THE JOB

God as Trinity dwells within our hearts. We often feel the "nudges" of the Spirit, to move us toward realizing our giftedness and generous serving of others. Saint Ignatius advises followers to do the Awareness Examen or Consciousness Examen each day, even if they have no time to do other spiritual practices. The Examen goes like this, after we settle in some sacred place in our bedrooms or living rooms: (1) Thank God for all gifts and benefits; (2) Ask for light to walk through the day again; (3) Review thoughts, words, acts, desires, feelings of receptive listening or resistance; (4) Express gratitude, sorrow, forgiveness; (5) Thank God for continued presence.

A five-minute "spiritual walk" is a healthy spiritual experience for us at any age.

54
God is Greater Than Our Hearts

I have been blessed by sharing friendship with a holy theologian for 40 years! Though he has been gifted with intellectual abilities, outstanding preaching skills, is reputedly (many clergy share this with me) the "best teacher we ever had," the Scripture he has often repeated to me was this one in 1 Jn 3:18-24: "Cecilia, God is greater than our hearts." So, of course I have been meditating on it for 40 years.

We are tempted sometimes to want God to answer our prayers—as we wish them answered. Yet, God knows our hearts and chooses to give us what is best for us, even if the answer to our prayers is "No."

We apply for the "perfect job" and have to accept instead what we think is "second best" or worse, and we question God's judgment. Later, we find out that we learn more in this second position than we would have in the first choice. The alternative also opens more doors to a more satisfying future, and even relationships, for us.

We lose a friend and-or companion who seemed to be a wonderful complement to our gifts, and we resent God's taking away such a marvelous gift, a person who seemed to fulfill our dreams for a perfect partnership. However, the "void" gives us a chance to examine our own talents, values, dreams, hopes for all tomorrows, qualities of friendships which would draw out of us our own giftedness, persons who would serve others with us instead of allowing us the satisfaction of a mutual "navel-gazing" relationship.

We feel God's "urges" to become more than we are, even to embark on a demanding vocation or profession that would serve others for a lifetime, though it may not be as remunerative as other careers. We ask God our usual "Why me?" But with God's looking deeply into our hearts until we also begin to do so, we allow ourselves to say "yes" and are flooded with the realization that we gain more than we give: travel, meeting outstanding people, high level education, cultural enrichment—and a sense of mission and personal worth.

God is indeed greater than our hearts. As we examine our aspirations, we begin to look deeply into our hearts—as God does!

55
Instant or Thriving Gratification

Please Don't Chop Down the Fig Tree

Theologically, the fig tree (*syke*) and the vine (*ampelos*), symbols also found in Micah 4:4 and Joel 2:22, are signs of God's blessings. In Luke's use of the fig tree tradition (13:6-9), the fig tree is not summarily cut down. It is allowed time for growth and change—to bear fruit. The promise of the gardener is this: the exhausted soil around the tree will be cultivated, fertilized, and cared for.

Is There a Crisis of Instant Gratification?

When we step back and look at U.S.A. culture, a culture that people from many nations seem to wish to emulate, we wonder if our propensity for instant gratification might have become a danger to our hope for loving collaboration to achieve a peaceful world. We eat fast food, heat up instant meals, stand in line for the brand-new iPhone, drive through car washes, want to offer our opinions on running the government, make quick judgments on the others' behaviors before we ask about motives or stresses or sufferings. Alas, at times we say angry hurtful words instead of thoughtfully finding out the other's position, make decisions quickly about breaking off relationships before we prayerfully and lovingly try to resolve differences, and too often in our nation a person uses a gun to "get back at" a slight or resolve a jealousy.

First Give Time, Cultivate, Fertilize, and Care For

I often meditate on God as ultimate Wisdom, Goodness, and Beauty. Seeking these attributes for ourselves seems to fit here. We can learn from our Loving God the Wisdom of the discipline of a "thriving" life-giving gratification: not having this food now but making a nourishing selection, not responding with the cutting word but trying to heal the distance. We can copy the Creator's Goodness by trying to see the 95% good in the person and letting go of the 5% that "bugs" us. We can search for God's Beauty in the lovely Spring daffodils, and the person who works by our side. We can give all the events, encounters, and decisions in our lives more time, cultivation, and care, so each moment of our lives can bear fruit—instead of wilting to irredeemable decay.

56
Everything I Have is Yours

ALWAYS PRESENT TO CREATE, FORGIVE, "SPOIL," AND LOVE

How often in Sacred Scripture does God remind His children that they are chosen, dear to God's Heart, taken back to a covenant relationship after they have committed some pretty serious transgressions (Isaiah 42:1, Is 43: 1, Hosea 11:1-4). Even more, the Psalms and other texts in the Hebrew Bible let us reflect on the ways God "spoils" us with lavish gifts (Psalm 104, Joel 2:19-27). But the best gift is a personal God who speaks of Love for each of us (Deuteronomy 4: 32-40, Song of Songs 2:8-17).

AMERICANS A "SELF-SERVICE" NATION

But we Americans are quite grown up. Receiving gratuitously without paying or returning the favor is not easy. Recall the first time we said to our parents, "I can do it myself!" Or the questioning when we did a favor for someone, and were asked, "Well, what do you want"? It is interesting that we have reached the "self-service" stage where we shop at IKEA and put the pieces of the dresser together ourselves. We buy groceries at Freddie's and we can check out in a self-service line. In most of our States we fill our own tanks with gas. And, how many family sit-down meals do we experience annually? This "do it yourself" way of living our everyday lives makes it difficult to ask for anything—of others, and even of God.

The Spirituality of Asking

Luke's Gospel is about a Prodigal, lavish, extravagant Father who says to each of us, "You are here with me always; everything I have is yours." If we ask! I realize that I need to "Practice what I preach," but the Gospel encourages the older son to ask for anything he wishes—not to get so caught up in duty, obedience, deadlines, legalistic behavior, and a humorless rigor that precludes his wanting to celebrate the return of his brother who has indeed committed some serious transgressions. Perhaps this is where we can give each other in our "self-serve" nation some community support: encouragement to believe these words, when we want or need something, "Ask and it shall be given to you." Because everything God has is ours—for the asking!

57
My Grace is Sufficient for You

Learning about the Catholic doctrine of GRACE changed my life! I think I was born "Mommy's Little Worry Wart." The oldest of six, I was responsible for their safety when we made camps in Tacoma's very dry Scotch Broom fields; I spent summers in an inner tube assuring that siblings did not drown in the Tualatin River; I was reluctant to stay overnight at friends' homes because something might happen to one of my brothers or sisters.

Ah, the memorable day that CCD teachers spoke about ACTUAL GRACE! God would give me "at the moment I needed it" grace to make that representation to the mayor, on behalf of the neighborhood kids. At age 13 I learned that I did not have to be the official worrier of the family or friends at school! During that precious summer I learned about ACTUAL GRACE.

In the Old Testament (Hebrew Bible) the words that are precursors of "Grace" speak of the unfailing duty of reciprocity between contracting parties (specifically God and human persons). In Luke's Gospel the Old Testament usage survives, but the salvific grace of Christians is linked with the person of Jesus. In Paul's Romans the element of gratuitousness is brought out. But, the really important reality about grace is this: God does not confer on us merely created gifts as tokens of love; but God communicates God's very Self and makes it possible for us to share in the nature of God. For us created beings to be endowed with God in a personal love which communicates God's Self is an unmerited favor on God's part. We cannot regard this Self-Communication as identical with our own human characters, as some hold ("We are God" idea); for our ability to accept this Gift of God's Self-Communication is also a free grace.

To boil this theological notion of grace down to the practical: Grace is both God's Self-Communication to us as gift which we can carry always; and also, God can offer a special "in-breaking" into our lives, guiding us when we need special help, like ACTUAL GRACE to do something. We recognize God in our neighbors, nod or bow, and pray, "Namaste, the God in me recognizes the God in you." And we live in the Self-Communicating Presence of a God Who is always ready to assist us "worriers" – or "former worriers."

58
Most Holy Body and Blood of Christ

Not many years ago, on the Feast of Corpus Christi, Catholics of many neighborhoods carried the Eucharist in Procession, stopping at "home-made" flowers-and-white-tablecloth altars enroute, singing the twenty verses of the Sequence of the Mass: *Lauda Sion*. (www.usccb.org-readings) We celebrated the reality of the words Jesus said to the Jewish crowds: *"I am the living bread that came down from heaven; whoever eats this bread will live forever; and the bread that I will give is my flesh for the life of the world."*

Father Raymond E. Brown suggested that this material was originally part of John's Supper Traditions, though John 6:51-58 situates it in the Bread of Life section. Each verse in this section follows the same pattern of referring first to eating the flesh and drinking the blood. Following this are the claims that it is necessary to eat His flesh and blood with a reference to Salvation. We recall when we read John that the Father sent the Son to give Eternal Life—and the Life which the Son has is the Father's own Life given to the Son; this type of relationship between Father and Son is extended to us who are believers. That's what we were celebrating in those processions, and truly what we celebrate on the Feast of Corpus Christi and every Mass where we receive again the Most Holy Body and Blood of Christ.

I heard yesterday a story about a student who raised his hand after the professor lectured on the Trinity. The professor asked,

"You have a question on the Trinity?" The student answered, "No, I understand that." And the professor walked over and knelt at the student's feet, saying, "You are the first one in history."

Possibly the same situation would occur if any of us tried to explain The Mystery of the radical transformation that takes place when we receive the Body and Blood of Jesus. Yet I can still recall my kneeling in the front row of Visitation Church in Tacoma, Washington, and watching in awe as a woman passed me, kneeling at the edge of the pew after receiving the Eucharist—her radiance "told" me that something miraculous had happened, and the experience moved me to anticipate the day of my First Holy Communion.

59
The Holy Spirit Helps Us "Get It"

They were confused, astounded, amazed because each one heard in his or her own language! (Acts 2:1-11)

Our Creator "carved out each of us" as skillfully as Michelangelo brought "David" out of a piece of flawed marble. And God's Spirit speaks to our hearts about ways we can best shape the Dream that God has for each of us. We hear God's unique message or call to us in different languages! When I listen to people in Spiritual Direction I hear the miracle of God's voice speaking to one as he plays his violin, another as she rocks her child, another as he hikes through the woods or skis down a mountain, another as she writes poetry or a thesis, another as he suffers a loss, and others as they kneel quietly in prayer or do walking meditation.

That God cares to speak to persons "in their own language" always leaves me awestruck. In the United States we see ourselves as terribly individualistic. Yet, we seem to have to copy the "latest" telephone, clothing style, car, haircut, music, short-cut speech jargon that everyone else has adopted. So, to actually believe that God is so sensitive to each of us that "our unique style" determines the ways God's message comes to each of us is simply an amazing (daily) Pentecost experience! Yet this kind of listening to God's unique way of speaking to us personally is a primary element in the art of discernment, of listening to the direction God is moving us at this stage of our lives.

If I could have any gift, I would beg for the Art of Listening. It's a hard gift to un-wrap in our world today, with: noise every place we go, expectations of others, interruptions to our stories, our own hurts and angers which are impediments to freedom, habits that block our ears from hearing the Good News and Bad News of Truth, our fears of Listening because we know that we would have to Respond. That is why we need daily to listen to the consoling words of Paul in 1 Corinthians 12, "To each individual the manifestation of the Spirit is given for some benefit" (ours, the world's)!

60
Calls and Responses

June is a month for weddings, vow ceremonies (consecrated life), ordinations (diaconate, priesthood), a month of "public yeses" to God's unique calls to holiness, through living a life commitment in Faith and Fidelity. Catholic and other Communities celebrate the "beginnings" and "jubilees" of these "yeses."

Not long ago I was advisor to students in Human Studies, Religion, and Ethics. A surprising number shared: "I think I had a call to be a sister-brother, but I didn't get encouragement. I was afraid to try. I got married. Now I'm a single parent, divorced, with 3 children. Don't get me wrong. I love my children. But, I wonder if I should have said 'yes' to that call." God still calls followers, from the 1st to 21st Centuries.

The CALL from God is often a subtle voice, heard as we: stroll by the ocean, pray, hear a homily, receive the Eucharist, listen to a question from a Sister or Brother who recognizes our gifts, volunteer in a hospice center. Also, in my case, when doors close: though I was engaged, wedding plans continued to get thwarted. Often, as Pentecost reminds us, the Spirit uses multiple (insistent) voices to get heard.

If we are Catholics, knowing the Spirit's GIFTS to us are for building up the Body of Christ clues us in to what kind of congregation suits us: health care as Sister of Providence or Alexian Brother, educator as Sister of the Holy Names or Christian

Brother, missionary as Medical Mission Sister or Maryknoll Brother, spiritual director as Cenacle Sister or Jesuit, work in communications as Benedictine Sister or Franciscan Friar. The path is similar for Jews and other Christians. Diverse needs are matched with a variety of gifts among many cultures in the USA. Parents, teachers, all in the Community need to encourage people as they search for the best use of gifts.

Though charisms-gifts are lavishly bestowed by a Loving Creator, they are for building up God's Community, creating a loving humane world. Yet, the UNEXPECTED REWARDS are many: most Sisters, Brothers, Priests and Ministers have Masters' or Doctoral degrees; are exposed to excellent retreats, liturgies, lectures, and concerts; can be with family who are ill or dying; get their own gifts "stretched" by serving others; and travel. As my Navy brothers say, "Join the convent and see the world."

61
Trinity: Once a Topic for Butcher, Baker, Candlestick Maker

In earlier centuries of Christianity the Trinity was a common topic of discussion. Theologian Catherine Mowry LaCugna, in *God for Us*, begins,

> *"... (A)t one time the doctrine of the Trinity was center of a vital debate, but Christianity and Christian theology seem to have functioned for several centuries with a doctrine of the Trinity relegated to the margins. Not until recently has this fundamental area of Christian theology begun to attract renewed interest... Trinitarian doctrine is not above all a theory about God's 'internal self-relatedness' but an effort to articulate the basic faith of Christians: 'In Jesus Christ, the ineffable and invisible God saves us from sin and death; by the power of the Holy Spirit, God continues to be altogether present to us, seeking everlasting community with all creatures'... The doctrine of the Trinity is... a teaching not about the abstract nature of God, nor about God in isolation from everything other than God, but a teaching about God's life with us and our life with each other."*

TRINITY IS COMMUNITARIAN.

That model is inspiration to women and men who choose to express their Love for God and their commitment to serve God's People within a community context. Each spring many people ask the "What's next?" question: "What kind of preparation will I need, to answer God's next call for me as lay minister, deacon, male or female religious, priest, married person, minister or pastor, or vocation to serve in public life or medicine or missions?" In summer we witness weddings of couples sacramentally committing themselves to a family community. And men responding to God's call to priesthood or diaconate within a Church community.

In past generations families "gave to God" one of their 6 to 10 children. Catherine Talia, OSU reflects on religious community:

> *"As women (and men) religious we spend our lives communally not individually, differentiated yet bonded. We find our strength in one another and work toward communal discernment and decision-making for the common good... We work to build human community and dare to be a Gospel presence... We embrace our broken world, the global community, and bring to it our years of experience, of listening with heart."*

All are called to create a healthy Planet Earth with a united loving human community "In the Name of the Father, and of the Son, and of the Holy Spirit."

JULY

62
An Understanding Heart

A wise woman who was traveling in the mountains found a precious stone in a stream. The next day she met another traveler who was hungry; the wise woman opened her bag to share her food. The hungry traveler saw the precious stone and asked her to give it to him. She did so without hesitation. The traveler left, rejoicing in his good fortune. He knew the stone was worth enough to give him food and security for a lifetime.

But, a few days later, he came back to return the stone to the wise woman. "I've been thinking," he said. "I know how valuable this stone is, but I give it back in the hope that you can give me something even more precious. Give me what you have within you that enabled you to give me this stone."

Sometimes it's not the wealth we have but what's inside us that others need. Solomon "got it," and asked God for that precious something inside: Wisdom, an Understanding Heart. We have read many "Solomon stories": The Velveteen Rabbit, Mother Theresa's *Do It Anyway* prayer, parables like the one above. All of them tell us that it often takes a long time to become wise, and by then knees creak, eyes weaken, pain is a daily companion, travels have taught us about the wisdom of people in other cultures, and sometimes things one has spent a lifetime gathering—are lost.

What is really important is this: knowledge and wisdom are not the same! We can gather all kinds of data on Google; we can read dictionaries on different topics; we can attend hundreds of lectures; we can pass our multiple-choice examinations with flying colors. But, to be wise we need to internalize what we know: apply it, pray about it, make it our own, use it for the benefit of others, put pieces of knowledge together in creative ways—for the good of humankind.

Solomon asked for an understanding heart that he might be able to govern wisely. His is our prayer: we need to ask God for Wisdom, for internalized knowledge, for this special grace to carry inner peace and integrity—and open our bag without hesitation, just as this wise woman offered her precious stone to a stranger.

63
Shema: Listen, Hear, Obey, Respond

Examining the original languages in Scripture can be instructive. The same word can have multiple meanings, in this case to "listen," "hear," "obey," and "respond." Recall the words cherished by Jews and Christians in Deuteronomy 6:4, The Great Commandment,

"Hear, O Israel...be careful to observe...that you may grow..."

THE LISTENING OF MARTHA AND MARY

The story of Martha and Mary, often misinterpreted I must say, is about "listening" and "responding." Carefully reading the Gospels helps us recognize the importance of Martha to the early Johannine community. She represents the Johannine community and leads that community through crisis; and as leader, she proclaims Jesus as "the Christ, the Son of God, he who is coming into the world" (John 11:27). Jews would understand "Christ," Gentiles would understand "Son of God," and Samaritans would understand "He who is to come." In the Gospel of John, Martha plays the role reserved for Peter in Matthew, Mark, and Luke, according to theologian Regina Coll. Though Peter proclaimed almost identical words and was rewarded with the promise of being the foundation Rock for the Church, Martha's Faith profession seems to have been lost in the shadow of Peter's.

Nevertheless, Martha was a V.I.P. in the early Church. Jesus, however, chides her for "losing her balance." Like many of us, she became "busy about many things" and forgot the importance of balancing ACTION with LISTENING to the voice of God in Jesus. To be effective, grounded, life-giving Christians we need to keep a balance of listening, hearing, obeying (God's Spirit-Voice), responding. In this case Mary "got it right," and sat listening to Jesus' words. Perhaps some would say that she too "lost her balance" on the other end of not responding to others' needs after she had the chance to listen and to hear.

But the story is meant to emphasize *shema*, LISTENING to Jesus and RESPONDING appropriately as a result. For us, that may mean balancing our calendars a little better: prayer when we first get up and also as we walk around the house or to our offices; making Sabbath a reality in our lives with Mass or Worship and Sabbath rest; listening to the voice of God and responding as freely as we can: at home, work, in the family, and in all life settings.

64
Hearing That Sower's Message

Mahatma Gandhi, though not a Christian, summarizes a hearing-response to which we can aspire: *"Ours will be a truly spiritual nation when we show more truth than gold, greater fearlessness than pomp of power and wealth, greater charity than love of self."*

Once my father tilled the back yard, and carefully planted vegetable seeds in neat north-south rows; but he didn't mark the rows with the empty seed packets. Later, my Mother was delighted to see the soil all tilled, ready for planting; she diligently planted vegetable seeds in east-west rows and didn't mark the rows with her empty seed packets. Result: a "crazy-quilt" garden!

Sometimes we are mystified that God plants seeds of Truth and Goodness and Beauty in the hearts of all people on earth—and even God must be surprised at the "crazy-quilt" results. As the Gospel tells us, some hear the Word without understanding. Others hear with joyous hearts, but the message doesn't take root. People filled with anxiety about life or greed for what the world can offer often find that the Word is choked out by other interests—often placed low on their priority scales until they are ill or a loved one is dying of cancer. Yet there are people of every culture and status in life who do hear, understand, internalize, live out the messages of the Word—and their lives yield a great deal of peace and happiness for themselves, and a hundredfold for those whom they love and serve.

How could it be that people like Hitler could enter a seminary and yet his Faith had not been rooted: he was responsible for the death of 6 million Jewish people. Yet Mother Teresa would choose to let the Word sink into the rich soil of her being, and search the gutters for the dying, in order to help them die with dignity, feeling loved and cared for.

The Creator-Sower speaks and hopes for a hearing: through Scripture, in events of Life, in the tilled soil of each being. We listen and respond differently—creating a confusing "Christian patchwork quilt" for our children, religious "searchers," and the hurting populations of the world. Yet, the Sower respects our HUMAN FREEDOM to use computers, cars, money, even our own words and actions to plant seeds of growth or death.

65
Freedom and Conscience

Listening to the Heart

The words in Deuteronomy are key to living in our complex world with what we call spiritual freedom: "This command that I enjoin on you…is not too mysterious and remote from you…it is something very near to you, already in your mouths and in your hearts; you have only to carry it out." Theologian Karl Rahner says conscience is the experience of freedom that makes us aware of our RESPONSIBILITY (think "response-ability"). The Biblical term for conscience is "heart" (Ezek 11, Rom 2, Jas 1, 2 Cor 4, Mt 5, Mt 12); so freedom of conscience that leads us to make free and responsible decisions is a pretty serious inner call for Jews and Christians—it infers a lifelong listening to one's heart where the Spirit "urges" us to move in the direction that will make us the best persons we can be and which is also life-giving for the "common good."

Reading and Responding to the Inner Voice of Conscience

Catholics had a 3-point guide about what constituted a serious "not listening" to conscience and freely choosing what was not good for oneself or others or God (they called it "sin"): (1) the act had to be a seriously bad act (taking a life or destroying someone's name, e.g.), (2) one had to have full knowledge that the act was evil (courts protect the mentally incompetent), and (3) one freely chose to carry it out anyway (force and fear inhibit freedom). But, life's choices are often not clearly "good" or "bad": sometimes one has to choose "the best good" among many good choices (going to college or staying home to help financially because a parent is unemployed); and the "least evil" among many bad choices (taking a medication with adverse side effects or accepting suffering and possible death). Spiritual direction and discernment have had a resurgence among Christians to spiritually support us in this world with many free choices.

God gifted us with intelligence and freedom. Our "thank you" for those gifts is living as a spiritually free person, informing out consciences through study, listening to the "not too mysterious and remote" Spirit, and trusting that "we only have to freely carry out" the decisions of our informed consciences.

66
The Problem of Evil

Jesus says to the crowds, *"Let them (wheat and weeds) grow together until harvest..."* Good and Evil. The problem of evil is and has been the most serious problem in our world. It is also the one serious objection to the existence of God!

When Thomas Aquinas wrote the *Summa*, he found only two objections to the existence of God: (1) the apparent ability of natural science to explain every experience without God; (2) the problem of evil.

Evil is not just an intellectual objection; we feel it; we live it. If God is all-good, all-wise, all-loving, all-just, all-powerful, why does God seem to be doing such a miserable job of keeping the world a good, safe place to live? Some thoughts for our contemplation:

First, evil isn't a thing, but it is a reality. Every "thing" God created is good. Evil is not a thing, but a wrong choice(s), and damage done from a wrong choice. Six million Jews were killed because of wrong choices and actions following them.

Second, the origin of evil is not the Creator of all beings but the creature's freely choosing sin, selfishness, greed. Whether the consequence of sin was a physical change in the world or only a spiritual change in human consciousness—whether "thorns and thistles" grew in the garden only after the Fall or were always there but were only felt as painful by the newly fallen consciousness—the connection between spiritual evil and physical evil is as close as the human soul and body, the "embodied soul."

Third, the solution to the problem of evil is not thought only, but the Person Jesus Christ, sent by the Father's Love to defeat the power of evil in human nature. The practical solution for us is to be the heart and hands of that Model and engage in the mop-up operations.

Fourth, suffering can work for the greater good of wisdom. Moreover, we learn to trust even fallible human beings, trust each other as well as God—like the child who jumps into the arms of the calling firefighter whom he does not see. No sane person wants evil, or hell, to exist; they seem unreal. So does Auschwitz. So does Calvary. But it remains true that "all things work together for good to those who love God."

67
Three-Stage Journey to Truth

We ask down-to-earth questions about profound human and spiritual development, about rejection of religion and about all of the Mysteries of life. We worry that our children, grandchildren, students, and friends no longer participate in Worship or the Eucharist, except at Christmas and Easter, Good Friday, weddings, and funerals. We are puzzled that the weddings of our younger relatives take place on a dune buggy, or white river raft, or at the Rhododendron Park. We also notice many older persons seem wrinkled but wise, and at peace with Life.

Matthew's Gospel today reminds us that "the Lord of Heaven and Earth has hidden these things form the wise and the learned." What happens spiritually to human beings, between the ages of 6 and 86?

The French philosophical theologian Paul Ricoeur offers a three-stage explanation of the journey to spiritual maturing.

In the First Stage of Naivete, we take religious belief or Scripture at face value. We read the text literally; we tend to obey the "letter of the law," we are satisfied with quick catechism-like answers, we adopt what "sister says" or "my dad told me, " we judge others from a "black and white" perspective, we look at right or wrong from extreme positions and find it difficult to accept moderate or pastoral positions.

In the Second Stage of Naivete, often beginning with high school and university, human beings inspect rationally the literal meanings of religion. They step back from the religious beliefs that are literal, black and white, rather fixed, and examine them critically. Thus, they begin to internalize religious truths, see where they fit their life experiences, and how to make them "their own" instead of those of their parents, teachers, friends, siblings. Sometimes it looks as if they reject everything we taught them.

In the Third Stage, what he calls "Second Naivete," Scripture and religious concepts are seen as meaningful symbols of deeper truths. We accept gracefully the myths and stories that we held as truths in the first stage, and recognize that we have passed through the critical distancing stage. But we no longer accept truths literally, even as presented by authority, but we interpret them for ourselves. We now assume personal responsibility for what we believe. We realize that these religious truths represent something more mysterious than the literal words or letter of the law. We act out of the truths we have internalized.

We have taken the journey to become mature believers of Truth and doers of Good.

68
Who Deserves Mercy?

Few of us would choose the ancient Book of Jonah as bedtime reading. Nevertheless, it is a relevant book for our day. The reluctant prophet Jonah is anything but a cardboard character; he seems to have a crabby disposition, he runs from reality when he does not like it, he struggles with notions of God as just and yet merciful. Especially he does not understand how God can extend free and unmerited mercy to people like the Ninevites!

Four scenes in the book tell the story. In chapters 1 and 3 the sailors and their captain, and the people of Nineveh, are led to believe in God—through, of all people, Jonah himself. Chapters 2 and 4 focus on Jonah and God, and death; in chapter 2 Jonah praises God for rescuing him from the great fish, delivering him from death, but in chapter 4 Jonah wishes for death, out of obstinacy and frustration.

Ah, we are led into the secret: the reason Jonah fled toward Tarshish was that he feared his efforts in preaching would have a positive effect, and he wanted nothing to do with the possible extension of divine mercy to these hateful, unworthy people! How many times have we used the words "he-she-they do not deserve..." as we speak about the generations of people on welfare, the games played by countries like Iran, the drunk drivers who think they are "safe" behind the wheel, those who treat people greedily and unjustly. We simply do not understand how a merciful God does not strike them down instead of poor people in countries hit by floods and storms like those in the story of Jonah. We are tempted to allow the same kind of frustration and obstinate pouting as did Jonah.

When Jonah says he is angry enough to die, God explains compassionately that He is concerned about the thousands of people in Nineveh who do not know their right hand from their left. As Sovereign Lord of all Creation, God asserts His freedom to save even Nineveh from destruction. My mother used to remind me, when I contested not getting my share in life, "Work as if all depends on you, but pray as if all depends on God." As individuals and as a nation, we do need to work as hard as we can to bring about justice in our nation and world; but, the Mystery of God's Mercy will always lie deep at the bottom of the ocean with the "great fish."

69
Do Not Judge by Appearances

When I was in graduate school I studied at the National Library in Washington DC and interacted with many homeless people as I walked from the train station. One morning I watched a man pull a grapefruit rind from the garbage and fill it with water from the fountain, drinking the water and eating left-over food from his paper bag lunch, before he rested on the library lawn. The next day I put a thermos with bars and other simple foods in my backpack and offered these to him. He thanked me, told me he was happy with what he had, and dismissed me—in elegant, well-educated, intelligent English! He gave me a lesson: do not judge by appearances.

That is the message of 1 Samuel too: Who knows the person God wants to select to carry out His mission? Ephesians continues to highlight this message: Everything exposed by the light becomes visible. Further, the long Gospel in John makes visible that God's actions are beyond our ability to "see the whole picture." The blind man, blind not because his parents sinned but so that the works of God might be made visible through him, was healed: "He opened his eyes."

We notice that people too often make snap judgments on appearances, without looking further into the event or transaction. Why does that person appear to be sad, angry, depressed, happy, defeated? What is behind the words that person used to describe a situation? Did that salesperson treat me rudely because I did not buy the more expensive item? All day long we listen to words, watch actions, and notice behaviors that may puzzle us.

It is not always possible to question everyone, instead of forming judgments on appearances alone. But, with our loved ones, friends, and colleagues, it may be far better to say simply, "I seem to notice some hesitation, or distress, or puzzlement in your response. Is there something you would wish me to clarify?" Too often we retaliate instead of engaging in dialogue—with individual persons and even among countries. And, too often acting on appearances can lead to broken relationships, divorce, and even wars.

What if we made it a rule for ourselves that: 1. We would not make snap judgments on appearances, and 2. We would not retaliate on this basis, that we would refuse to treat others as we have just been treated by a person who may be hurting, angry, or suffering a loss and striking out at someone who will not cease to love him or her.

70
Why Is It So Hard to Ask for Help?

She had just reached the age of 65, had retired, lost her husband of 30 years, moved to senior living, and had a "scary" eye surgery to repair a wrinkle in the retina.

"Why is it so hard to ask for help?" The question arose when she needed to ask for a friend to drive her to a doctor's appointment and a meeting. We Americans have grown up with a "pull yourself up by your own bootstraps" Manichean (early Church heresy) attitude and we are surrounded by an atmosphere of individualism. At age 3 we may have declared adamantly, when our parents tried to assist us with dressing, "I CAN DO IT MYSELF."

Strange behavior for all Christians who pray daily, "Our Father...give us each day our daily bread...forgive our sins...for yours is the Kingdom, the Power and the Glory." Jesus sent women and men disciples to "heal the sick...raise the dead...expel demons...the gift you have received, give as a gift" (Mt 10). When the disciples asked, "When did we see You hungry ...thirsty... away from home... naked...ill?" Jesus responded simply: "As long as you did it for one of my sisters or brothers, you did it for me" (Mt 25).

It takes a lot of living to learn that a collaborative community (pooling of gifts)—family, Church, workplace—achieves far better results than does our trying to accomplish a task or a mission all alone. We speak the theological words "Body of Christ" often, and we celebrate Body of Christ daily with many grains of wheat blended together in the One Bread and many grapes pooling to create the One Wine. Asking for help is part of our social nature.

We can use different gifts at various stages of our lives, our successive "new me's." Younger people often resist the wisdom or assistance of anyone older than they. Older persons want to continue doing things their way, even when that is no longer safe. What if we sat down together—as family, as parishioners, as cohorts in the workplace, as friends, as neighbors, AS HUMAN BEINGS IN COMMUNITY—and asked each person to speak about the gifts that God has given her or him, "the gifts that were given and which were meant to be given back to the Community" as Matthew's Gospel expressed it?

71
Mary Magdalene and the Other Marys

James Carroll wrote an article for the Smithsonian titled "*Who Was Mary Magdalene*"? (with the sub-heading, "*From the writing of the New Testament to the filming of The Da Vinci Code, her image has been repeatedly conscripted, contorted, and contradicted.*") That leaves us with the only evidence on which we Catholic Christians can really count: According to the New Testament, who was Mary Magdalene? Mary was a very common name in New Testament times, held by a number of women in the canonical Gospels. The reception history of Mary Magdalene has been greatly affected by different interpretations as to which biblical references actually refer to her, beyond those where she is identified by the toponym "Magdalene." In the gospels several women come into the story of Jesus with great energy, including erotic energy. There were Mary the Mother of Jesus; Mary of Bethany, sister of Martha and Lazarus (Lk 38-42 and John 11). Also, Mary the mother of James and Joseph, and Mary the wife of Clopas. Then there are three unnamed women who are expressly identified as sexual sinners and they have become part of the design—the woman who wipes Jesus' feet with ointment, a Samaritan woman whom Jesus meets at a well, and an adulteress whom Pharisees haul before Jesus to see if he too will condemn her. All of these Marys make it difficult to unravel the tapestry of Mary Magdalene from these knotted threads, of legends about Mary Magdalene.

In the four Gospels, Mary Magdalene is nearly always distinguished from other women named Mary by adding "Magdalene" (η Μ α γ δ α λ η ν ή) to her name. Traditionally, this has been interpreted to mean that she was from Magdala, a town thought to have been on the western shore of the Sea of Galilee. Luke 8:2 says that she was actually "called Magdalene." In Hebrew מגדל Migdal means "tower", or "fortress"; in Aramaic, "Magdala" also means "tower" or "elevated, great, magnificent."

The real Mary Magdalene of the Gospels actually fits well the Mission of who we are today: she knew about service to others and keeping them in the loop, she knew about inclusion; she knew about friendship; she knew about fidelity even when life looked desolate. For Mary Magdalene was a faithful friend of Jesus, one who hung in—according to the Gospels—during Jesus' public ministry as a disciple (Luke 8:1-2, Mark 16:9), as a witness at the foot of the Cross during the Crucifixion (Matthew 27:56, Mark 15:40, John 19:25), as one of the women who brought spices to anoint Jesus at the burial site (Mt 27:61, Mt 28:1, Mk 16:1), as a witness who found the tomb empty after the Resurrection (Mt 28:1, Mk 16:9, Lk 24, Jn 20:1), and as the first apostle to report the Resurrection to the rest of the disciples after Jesus' private appearance to her (Jn 20:16, Mk 16:9, Mt 28:9). Mary Magdalene was not afraid to be a friend! No matter what the personal cost.

The deep sacrificial friendship that Mary Magdalene had for Jesus has not only been intertwined with the many "Mary" stories of Christian history, but it has also been misinterpreted, calling her the secret wife of Jesus and the mother of his fate-burdened daughter—as well as other rather sad fictions about their relationships. Sometimes we judge true friendships harshly or at least suspiciously. Maybe there is a lesson to learn here, from Mary Magdalene's long-lasting friendship with Jesus. Deep and lasting friendships allow us to serve as disciples, to witness suffering, to rejoice at Resurrection…and Life!

I love Chapter 6 of the Book of Sirach (Ecclesiasticus) on true friendship:

> A faithful friend is a sturdy shelter; the one who finds such, finds a treasure.
>
> A faithful friend is beyond price; no sum can balance his worth.
>
> A faithful friend is a life-saving remedy; such a one fears God and finds.
>
> For the one who fears God behaves accordingly; and one's friend will be like oneself.

Let us often remember Mary Magdalene, one who had the privilege of calling Jesus... FRIEND.

AUGUST

72
Who Am I?

Jesus asks, "Who do you say that I am?" In the Gospels He unfolds His identity; during the Passion, He admits Who He Is to His abusers. The point is: Jesus knew Who He Was; the Word of God was there from the Beginning (Proverbs 8; John 1).

There is a reflective, significant article, "*Don"t Send Your Kid to the Ivy League Schools,*" by William Dersiewicz, in the *New Republic* and other journals. Author of *Excellent Sheep: The Miseducation of the American Elite and the Way to a Meaningful Life*, and a former professor at Yale, the author is worth reading. He makes the point that few of these graduates see college as a larger project of intellectual discovery and development. He claims that they tend to place their own interests first—not the common good. They do not tend to "think service." They are inclined to do what they have to do to get a "better return on investment."

The observations may sound a little harsh. But his examination shows that education in many quality private colleges, or fine public colleges, have empowered students to ask questions, create new horizons for themselves, learn who they are—instead of "measuring up," getting superior grades on tests, or learning what they need to know in order to take the next step up the financial ladder. Names of young entrepreneurs, founders, inventors, discoverers of cures for disease, and yes, saints, cross my mind. I chose a small liberal arts college, now Marylhurst University. When I went to a large public university for a graduate degree, I was asked by professors, "Where did you learn to think and write"?

Jesus' patient questioning about His identity, in Matthew's Gospel, raises questions for us as well. Not only do we need to ask, "Who is Jesus for me" but also "Who am I for Jesus?" The entirety of Mark's Gospel is about Jesus' gradual revelation of Who He Is to a group of Apostles who just "did not get it" until they looked back on years of interaction with Him.

Education happens with interactions among significant others—parents, teachers, God in prayer—and with our asking new questions: about God, Life, Ourselves, Others, Cultures, Religions, the World. Universities that "fit" the nature of our children, which free them to discover their own gifts and identities and possibilities for service, are worth searching out! Meaningful education moves each person to the project of intellectual discovery and personal development.

73
Have in You the Same Attitude as Jesus

Someone asked me to teach her how to forgive those who hurt her long ago through narrow and judgmental words and actions, and how to listen to boring table topics that wasted her time and are just a little hard to digest. Perhaps there are no pat responses, even though I am certain that the desire alone to forgive and accept would be pleasing to God. St. Paul must have had a lot of confidence in the Philippians to request: "Be of the same mind, with the same love, united in heart...have the same attitude that is also in Christ Jesus."

Maybe Philippians 2:1-5 is the mirror through which we need to experience people who bore their audiences with talk about the latest operation or the dog Muffy, the boastful who interrupt conversations by "playing one-up-man-ship," the mean-spirited who have cutting remarks for every laudatory remark we offer about another person. In Philippians, one of my favorite books because it so clearly puts me in my place and serves as an examination of consciousness (or conscience), Paul goes on to remind us: "If there is any encouragement in Christ, any solace in love, any participation in the Spirit, any compassion and mercy, complete my joy by being of the same mind (as Jesus)...do nothing out of selfishness or out of vainglory, humbly regard others as more important than yourselves, looking out for the interests of others."

One of the spiritual practices that St. Ignatius proposed was daily examination of consciousness; he valued it so highly that he suggested that we carry out this practice even if we had no time during the day for others. So, here it is again, in short form:

Before retiring we spend about five minutes reviewing the day, walking with Jesus or God or one's Wisdom figure. Experience again the "yuk" and "yum" moments (my niece's words): moments when we were selfish, hasty, mean, pompous; and also, the moments when we were loving, grateful, sincere, helpful. Then, simply talk to God about the day, perhaps breathing a prayer for forgiveness as well as a prayer of thanksgiving. This examination of consciousness helps us form a habit of putting on the attitude of Jesus.

74
Bible's Wisdom Literature Speaks to Our Time

Ecclesiastes (Greek) or *Qoheleth* (Hebrew) is quoted at Weddings, Funerals, and human events, especially Qoheleth 3:1-8, "For everything there is a season, and a time for every matter under Heaven: A time to be born, and a time to die...." The Wisdom Writers (Proverbs, Job, Ecclestes [Qoheleth], Ecclesiasticus [Sirach], Wisdom; sometimes Song of Songs [Canticle of Canticles] and Wisdom Psalms) reflect on the realities of everyday life. Job helps us see meaning in suffering and death and transformation. Proverbs offers wise advice about raising children for professional life. Sirach 6 has an insightful section on human friendship. Canticle of Canticles is a touching poem on human love and passion. Wisdom describes the qualities of Wisdom to which we aspire, especially as we deal with the complexities of our world. Qoheleth, the thinker, truly reflects on "everything under the heavens" and addresses all of us who are skeptics—but concludes in words of a believer: "The end of the matter; all has been heard. Love God, and keep the commandments; for that is the whole duty of everyone."

Perhaps because I was the little kid who constantly asked "Why?" I chose the Wisdom Literature for doctoral study—and fell in love with those writers, for they had so much to say to the human condition of the 20th and 21st centuries. Our children ask questions posed by Qoheleth (Ecclesiastes) and tell us that they embrace a Spirituality but not a Religion

People are searching passionately for a love that is deep and enduring and rooted in God, portrayed for us by the Canticle of Canticles. And finding true friendship, intimacy, and generous self-giving, in a world where many are guided in their decisions by self-interest, is Sirach's story. Women will "stand taller" when they see themselves mirrored in the book of Wisdom. Victims of cancer, heart disease, kidney failure, and other physical sufferings—as well as those who are sustaining painful losses of loved ones, jobs, homes—can be consoled by Job's words: "I have uttered what I did not understand...heard of you by the hearing of the ear, but now my eye sees You."

Do read the Wisdom Literature! It speaks to our lives today!

75
Hope in Miracles of Healing

You may have heard people declare, "If God is so good, why didn't He heal my child-spouse-friend-parent-colleague? And, why did God let all of those people get killed by a tornado-earthquake-flood-bomb? I'm through with God and Church and all that religion stuff." In the Bible Elijah brings an only son of a widow back to physical life; Jesus asks a young man to rise from the dead; and He too gives him back to his widowed mother. God can indeed perform physical healings, directly or through holy people we call saints. In fact, often these miracles of physical healing have been used as evidence that a person might be canonized as a "Saint" by the Church. But God does not usually intervene when I, a drunk driver, take a powerful instrument called an automobile, and kill someone with it.

How do we explain things like such "accidents," or "ontic" evils (physical disasters), as the theologians call them? And how do we account for mass killings by angry-mentally ill-yes, evil persons? The honest truth is, we can't—though scientists are studying the DNA of criminals to derive physiological answers. I used to admit to ministerial students when we tried to answer such questions, "Perhaps one of the biggest 'mistakes' God made was to create human beings with free will: they can do the greatest good for other human beings, and they can also choose to do terrible evils." We are free to love God with our whole heart and soul; and love our neighbors to the point of giving up our lives for them.

We are also free to participate in God's miracles of healing beyond the physical: by listening and loving hard-to-reach people into wholeness, by not "giving up" on persons who seem to be heading toward tragedy by using drugs, by teaching a teen or immigrant person some skills for employment, by walking with a dying person toward a peaceful death, by giving someone the power to forgive a grave injustice so emotional scars can heal.

The great Truth in Deuteronomy and the Gospels is this: we human beings can use our free wills to heal a broken world, or we can shatter both world and people!

76
The "New Normal" Spirituality: Seek the All-Around-Us-God

Isaiah asks us to "Seek the Lord while He may be found." And, our Catholic Theology reminds us in many ways that God is present in each of us, and in every created reality that exists or has existed. Catholic Christian *Panentheism* is the belief that the One God (monotheistic) interpenetrates every part of nature and timelessly extends beyond it. (*Pantheism*, on the other hand, holds that the divine is synonymous with nature; some "I am God" believers have internalized this philosophy.)

Finding time for God, during this decade, can be difficult: our 24-hour days need to stretch to listen and respond to our spouses, children, grandchildren, colleagues at work, Church, maintenance of home and car, friends, neighbors, rest, meals, leisure—sigh! Still, if God is present in all, interpenetrates as theologians and philosophers put it, the search is: "Where do I meet the All-Around-Us-God in every moment of my life?" Catholics have often used the phrase, "finding God in all things," and Buddhist philosophy uses the term "living mindfully."

And, that's it! The "new normal" of spirituality for many of us means we seek God in the words of a spouse, we thank God for the energy of the children who are driving us crazy with their noise, we pray a psalm about the Autumn leaves, we pet with reverence the dog which begs for treats, we respect the neighbor's property even if his leaves fall on our lawns, we listen patiently to the person who loves to air grievances or her brand of political truths. And, we breathe short prayers of thanks or requests for the Spirit's assistance as we walk toward our cars, take bathroom breaks, wait for the dentist, watch a Little League game, sit by as a friend makes up her mind to buy that dress, wonder if that guy will ever quit bragging, or take a coke or scotch break before dinner. Some people have called this "spirituality on the run."

All of these "God moments" we can collect once a week, as the praying Community comes together for the Eucharistic Liturgy or Worship Service. God is truly present in me, us, all creation, our activities—we need only to seek, and acknowledge, the All-Around-Us-God.

77
Thirsting for God

Jeremiah experienced a fire burning in his heart! And the Psalmist expressed in Ps 63, "My soul is thirsting for the Living God. When shall I see God's Face?" The Fathers of the Church spoke of our hunger and thirst for God, as did believers in the many Religious Traditions, as they told or wrote of their yearnings for encounters with their Supreme Beings.

St. Augustine wrote simply, "Our hearts are restless 'til they rest in Thee."

The human heart and mind and soul and body—one's entire being—reaches out for what philosophers and theologians call THE GOOD, both apparent and ultimate good. In our lives we have reached out for many GOODS. Some helped us grow into more loving, wise, giving, professional, interesting, beautiful, large-hearted people. Other choices of GOODS led us down paths of narcissism, addiction, ignorance, judgmentalism, anti-Semitism, anti-gay or anti-black prejudice, anti-feminine or anti-male positions—positions which have shrunk our world views or even led to what was destructive to others or to us.

From Genesis we recall the Creator, looking on creation, pronouncing each reality GOOD. When we reach out to any GOOD we believe at the time that it is GOOD FOR US, or at least for our momentary satisfaction. In our culture, where choices are ever-available to us and peer pressure moves us toward experimenting with heroin, prescription drugs, making money at the price of depriving someone, harming someone's good name so we might seem important, choosing other options than Worship or Eucharistic Liturgy on Sunday—the temptation to choose the immediate instead of the delayed satisfactions is just a heartbeat away.

All these occasions of reaching out toward or choosing what we believe is GOOD FOR US are indications of our thirst and hunger for the ULTIMATE GOOD, God, THE CREATOR OF ALL GOODS. People take many roads to good during a lifetime, some productive and some destructive. We have known that people choose rough roads that lead nowhere for decades, and one day do find the only GOOD that fills the human heart, God. Think again of Augustine.

We have one great consolation, as we try to satisfy our thirsting hearts: The Hound of Heaven is pursing us more steadily than we are searching the highways and valleys to satisfy the spiritual hunger, all the goods of our day.

78
A Tiny Whispering Sound

Why is it that the last thing we find, when we are searching for something, seems to be the most obvious? We find a satisfactory article when we shop, but we look at all other stores which carry such an article; then, we return where we started. We search for an answer to a question and find that the answer is in the book that seemed to jump off the shelf and ask us to read it. The keys that are "lost" were in the place where we usually set them.

Elijah did not find the Lord in the heavy wind, earthquake, or fire—but in a tiny whispering sound. In the Gospel, when the wind died down, the disciples recognized, "Truly, you are the Son of God." Often our seeing and hearing the Presence of God happens when we listen for the still small voice we encounter: spouses, children, pastor and parishioners, surprises God sends, the driver in front of us, the fragrance of the grass we mow, the ripe apple ready to fall from the tree, waves of the ocean, stars at night, cool lake water, a favorite pet—even the situations that hurt, the killings in the wars that shock us to the core, the pain of loss through death or divorce, misunderstandings with friends, the tragedies we experience, or the sadness of mental or physical illness.

In our quiet moments we remember that God is truly a Living Presence in all of Creation. When we pray for an hour at Adoration, we encounter the Real Presence in the Eucharist. When we do walking meditation, the colorful flowers "shout" God's name. When we doubt our worth, we recall that we are Temples where the Trinity dwells. When we are too discouraged to listen to the news about Africa, or Palestine, or Syria, we can try to hear Jesus calling us to bear in mind that Our God is a Presence in all that is. Maybe we can smile feebly and hear Jesus say from the boat, "O you of little faith, why did you doubt?"

But, then it is so obvious that the God Who Creates is also the Provident God who holds all of reality in an intimate embrace. This has to be so, or we would no longer exist.

79
They All Ate and Were Satisfied
Matthew 14

Two parents, two brothers, three sisters: a Baby Ruth candy bar divided into eight pieces. "Hey, Cissy, what's a half of a half of a half?"

That's how my brother, Edward, always a person who followed the rules of strict justice, learned fractions from his Big Sis.

Jesus told His Disciples that there was enough food for all the people, no need to send them away to scrounge for themselves. Instead, the disciples were to share what they had, five loaves and two fishes; not only did their resources prove to be enough—there were twelve wicker baskets of leftovers.

In moral theology we speak of general (distributive and commutative) and retributive justice. Justice, as one of the cardinal virtues (prudence, justice, fortitude, temperance), means the giving to all beings, their rights. In this sense one's rights as a human person confers a claim on another. To make this concrete, distributive justice happens between community and individual; it gives honors and imposes burdens. Commutative justice happens between an individual and another individual. When an injustice is done, retributive justice is expected.

Distributive justice requires that ecclesiastical leaders, educational authorities, trustees of charities, managers of corporations, wealthy persons, and judges protect fundamental human rights, and preserve the common good. It also means that, if we have millions of dollars, jobs, or food that would lie in the field or go into the ocean, that we share with those who do not have jobs, money to live on, and food to sustain life. Commutative justice respects person and property with regard to another's space, buying and selling, renting and leasing, payments and deposits. When property is destroyed, or a person's good name has been injured, retributive justice is expected from the moral person.

Greed on the part of one party, and scarcity on the part of others, does not add up to Justice as the Constitutions express it: right to life, liberty, and the pursuit of happiness. Parishioners witness to the virtue of Justice when we downsize and work diligently at projects for those in need—in order that others may be blessed with what they have a right to, EDUCATION FOR LIVES THAT THRIVE, THAT BASIC HUMAN NEEDS ARE SATISFIED AND THAT THESE SISTERS AND BROTHERS ARE NOT LEFT ON THE MARGINS OF SOCIETY.

80
Mary, Hope and Comfort for Pilgrim People

A Sunday is "sandwiched" between two feasts of Mary: Assumption on August 15 (Holy Day of Obligation) and Queenship of Mary on August 22. Vatican Council II placed Mary in *Dogmatic Constitution on the Church*, the first and major document: "Mary has by grace been exalted above all angels and humanity to a place after her Son, as the most holy Mother of God who was involved in the mysteries of Christ; she is rightly honored with a special cult by the Church."

It was November 1, 1950, that Pius XII defined the Assumption of Mary to be a dogma of faith, though many of the Eastern and Western churches have held steadily to this doctrine since the sixth century: "We pronounce, declare and define it to be a divinely revealed dogma that the immaculate Mother of God, the ever-Virgin Mary, having completed the course of her earthly life, was assumed body and soul to heavenly glory." The pope proclaimed the dogma only after broad consultation with bishops, theologians, and laity.

Pius XII, in his encyclical letter of October 11, 1954 granted the unanimous desire of the faithful and their pastors, and instituted the feast of the Queenship of Mary, thus giving sanction to a devotion that had already been practiced by many throughout the world who acknowledged Mary as the sovereign Mother of heaven and earth. That is, Church Fathers, Doctors, and Popes through the centuries have given authoritative expression to this truth. The crowning testimony to this common belief is expressed in the wonders of art, architecture, and the teaching of the liturgy. Moreover, the Laity recognized the queenly dignity of the Mother of "The King of Kings and Lord of Lords," and Theologians saw as fitting title that of Queen since she is so closely associated with the redemptive work of her Son.

Not only Catholics, but also other believers, look to Mary as a prototype of fidelity, dignity, integrity, and universal love and concern for all human beings. It occurs to me that we may wish to search the Scriptures, websites, museums, literature, poetry, art forms, and other sources for ways that women and men have, through the centuries, portrayed Mary, Mother of Jesus, and Mother of All Pilgrim People.

81
A Big Heart Open to God

That's the title of *America Magazine's* online interview (www.americamagazine.org-pope-interview) with Pope Francis. The Gospel reminds us of the rewards of the poor man, Lazarus, who listened to Moses and the prophets, and was carried away by angels to the bosom of Abraham. Named after St. Francis, the poor one, Pope Francis also listened to Moses and the prophets, and the Christian Saints, and chose the way of simplicity: an apartment in the Casa Santa Maria, simple furniture, an icon of St. Francis, a state of Our Lady of Lujan (patron saint of Argentina), a crucifix, a statue of St. Joseph, and a small workspace. In our land of paying for extra storage units for all we collect during the decades, perhaps his manner of life, expressed in this interview, can be a meditation and model for us.

We unveil the Richness and Mystery of God slowly. Pope Francis reflects: "Abraham leaves his home without knowing where he was going... All of our ancestors in the faith died seeing the good that was promised, but from a distance...Our life is not given to us like an opera libretto, in which all is written down, but it means going, walking, doing, searching, seeing...We must enter into the adventure of the quest for meeting God; we must let God search and encounter us."

He adds: "If the Christian is a restorationist, a legalist, if he-she wants everything clear and safe, then he-she will find nothing. ...Those who today look for disciplinarian solutions, those who long for an exaggerated doctrinal 'security,' those who stubbornly try to encounter a past that no longer exists—they have a static and inward-directed view of things...Even if the life of a person has been a disaster, even if it is destroyed by vices, drugs or anything else—God is in this person's life."

We can pray for this balance Pope Francis exhibits, pastorally, intellectually, theologically, culturally, artistically: seeking Wisdom, Goodness, and also Beauty in the writings of Dostoevsky, the art of Caravaggio and Chagall, the music of Mozart, and the movies of Fellini. Yes, here is a Pope who is a genuine human being who teaches us, as did Jesus of Nazareth, how to live and love and enjoy and serve!

SEPTEMBER

82
New Beginnings

Many Americans, and others throughout the world, experience September as a time of New Beginnings. Schools begin a new academic year. High school and college athletes suit up for football season. Merchants offer new merchandise for students, but also for the Fall Season. People take Summer clothing to the cleaners, storing them in moth balls to keep Winter moths away. Even the leaves begin to fall, knowing that soon branches and trunks will go to sleep for the colder season before they sprout new life in Spring.

The sign in the air is this: we have another chance to begin afresh, to get better grades, to wear new comfortable clothing, to try new ventures with a new breath of courage, to look ahead with hope and not back with regret. The phenomenon is in our blood.

Think of the many times Jesus said, “Stand up and walk. Your sins are forgiven.” Peter was given three new chances to erase his former denials, with the declaration of his love and the commitment to serve the People of God. Books of both the Hebrew Bible OT) and the Christian Bible (NT) repeat the message over and over: My People, I love you with an everlasting love, I take you back into my embrace, I forgive you, and I send you forth to a new beginning—a wider embrace of and service of other human beings, even your current enemies. Think of Hosea, Jeremiah, Isaiah, and from our human beginnings, Genesis.

The loving Begin-Again-My-People-God, who calls us to *Metanoia*, a deep change of heart we translate as conversion, has been insistent about new beginnings since the creation of humankind. We celebrate in our Sacraments this deep reality of starting afresh, over and over. The Sacrament of Reconciliation sends each of us forth with assurance of forgiveness of all that blocks our using the gifts of the Creator, so we can love the Lord Our God with our whole heart and soul and mind—and our neighbors as ourselves. The Eucharist fills us with the spiritual energy and presence of Jesus the Christ to fulfill our life's mission in ever-new ways.

It's time to remember that the days of September are invitations to put a foot on the starting line and run with our faces to the wind, with a sense of having been given a fresh chance for a New Beginning.

83
Spirituality of Work

A spirituality of work is founded on our belief in sacramentality, for everything that is, is holy. Our hands consecrate everything our work lets us touch in the service of God, God's People, and the world around us. Cleaning the house brings order to the world; watering a drooping tomato plant breathes life into the earth under our feet; writing a term paper draws on the wisdom that has existed in the universe throughout history; splinting a broken bone facilitates new growth and re-creates tissue with the energy of the Source of all Life. A spirituality of work calls on our unique creativity. We design mouth-watering salads, frame new houses, organize programs for the homeless, gather people to co-labor for peace and justice. We put our own "autograph" on the shaping of a healthier, happier, holier universe.

A spirituality of work draws us out of ourselves to "be the persons we were meant to be," leading us to be persons of compassion and wisdom. We insert ourselves into the human race in ways that reduce our destructiveness and produce life-giving effects wherever our presence and efforts are felt. At the same time, we begin to realize that we possess a "me" that we like, that is unique and worthwhile, that is valuable to the whole of humanity...and that we are not living our lives alone or in vain.

A spirituality of work draws us deeply into the efforts to create human community. In the process of "col-labor-ation" it dawns on us that every work in which we engage has an effect on somebody else. It becomes real to us that we are connected to the person who repairs our sinks, cleans our offices, does our lab work at the hospital, preaches about the Gospel for Sunday, rocks the baby at the children's hospital, begs for food because unemployment left her homeless, or assumes responsibility as a politician. The poor are often poor because we need to distribute the world's goods more effectively; the lonely are alone because we cannot find time for a short visit.

We realize that our work is God's work. It is not yet finished, because God is waiting for us to finish it.

84
Family, Century 21

At Graduation students introduce me to their families: "I would like you to meet my Father...Step-Mother...Partner...Half-Sister...Older Brother...Adopted Sister...." I step into a different world than that in which I grew up: My grandparents raised 13 children and remained together until Grandfather died in Grandmother's arms at age 78. My parents raised 6 children and celebrated their 56th anniversary before my Father died of lung cancer at age 77, and my mother later at 84.

In our world of diversity, politicians, ministers, and other persons speak, on television, in journals, in all forms of media, about "family values." It is an elusive term that could use a focus, especially in a world where families were not raised with a clear sense of ethical values.

This leads us to reflect on the "family values" of that Holy Family that lived 2,000 years ago. Certainly, Joseph took Jesus to Temple to learn to pray and to socialize with the Jewish Community; he taught him a trade, one which would enable him to be self-sufficient; and the many examples that Jesus used in telling parables are indicative of the reality that He must have visited farmers, shepherds, tax collectors, astrologers, and women and men from many professions. During the first 12-30 years of His life, Jesus seems to have spent much time with His Mother, as well as women that sought her wisdom. Jesus learned values and skills for His ministry: healing the sick, teaching the un-learned, listening to parents of sick children, soothing the troubled, forgiving prostitutes and sinners. When I was in Peru, single women engaged in prostitution at night, in order to feed their children; they left their children with the Sisters each evening, so their loved ones would not be abused and traumatized if they were left alone in the streets!

Pope Francis' words, "Who am I to judge?" may need to be a mantra for us as we are introduced to what constitutes "family" and "family values" in this 21st Century. We are not called to be judges of others and their families, but to embrace the values and learn the skills of the Holy Family. These values of the Holy Family still "fit" after 2000 years: seek Wisdom, teach children to pray, stretch relatives and friends to embrace a broader world view, heal the sick, teach the un-learned, soothe the troubled, and forgive others—love all members of the Human Family.

85

But I've Got Promises to Keep

(Robert Frost)

"I promised…" said the Lord. And, no matter what our Ancestors did, their Loving Creator figured out a way (or called Prophets) to invite them to repent and to return to the embrace of God. God kept, and keeps, promises!

Those of us who are counselors, pastoral care providers, educators, medical specialists, or contributors of care and healing for children and adults, know all-too-well that, in the case of these sufferers, promises have not been kept. Trust was broken. For these persons, first responses are often those of mistrust, defensiveness, unwillingness to believe our words, and even violent striking out or negative retorts. They find it hard to pray aloud with a group, to share their ideas in a communal setting, to create friendships of equality, to reveal who they are, and to trust that God loves them unconditionally and is always present to suffer with and to assist them in achieving their dreams and hopes for the future.

As a loving community, we have the privilege of being God's presence to each other—for few of us have had most promises to us fulfilled. We can listen deeply to another person's pain and disappointment and thereby serve as an agent of healing. We can keep our promises (or let the person know as soon as possible why we will be unable to do so, or to offer an alternative) and not say lightly (and fail to follow through), "O sure, I'll be on the committee" or "I'll be there for you." By honoring our promises to children, spouses, friends, co-workers, we re-build trust for persons, communities, work settings, Churches, and even nations—where we seem at this time in history to be suffering from a "crisis of disbelief."

Christians sing often, "Let us build the City of God..." Perhaps our challenge at this time in history is to re-build the City of God, in our families where some members have had promises broken many times before our paths crossed their lives, in our nation where politicians appear to promise everything but the sky if it will win the election, and even in our Church where broken promises have led to decades of broken hearts and pain. We have promises to keep!

86

Ever-Ancient Ever-New Covenant

We remember "hurts" when significant people failed to keep promises to us. Those promises were covenants to us! That's right: the covenant parties can be individuals, families, states, kings, or God; we expect benefits, rewards, blessings, or sanctions for keeping or breaking covenants.

In the Old Testament (Hebrew Bible) and New Testament we read of several covenants with God:

- Noah (God promised not to destroy the whole human race)
- Abraham (God promised that his descendants would be numerous, become a great nation, inherit the promised land, and that other nations would be blessed in him or through his offspring)
- Moses (God promised a reciprocity of relationship, "I will be your God; you will be my people.")
- David (God would establish a royal dynasty through his descendants; his son would build God's "house")
- Jeremiah (God would make a new covenant, God's law would be written in the hearts of people)
- Jesus, Son of God ("This cup that is poured out for you is the new covenant in my blood.")

When God's People did not keep their part of the Covenants, the Prophets called them to task, to repent, to return to the

Covenant relationship. They listened and responded, and a merciful God took them back. God keeps His side of the covenant. As the prophet Hosea 11:4 says: "I drew them with human cords, with bands of love; I fostered them like one who raises an infant to his cheeks; though I stooped to feed my child, they did not know that I was their healer."

The Hebrew word *shema* means both "to listen, hear" and "to obey, respond, grant a request." You recall the words of Deuteronomy 6:4 expanded in Matthew 22:34-40: "Hear…you shall love the Lord, our God, with all your heart, all your soul, all your strength," and Matthew added, "and love your neighbor as yourself."

Covenant People of God, we need make only ONE New Year's resolution. To listen (to the end of everyone's sentence). To listen to spouses, children, friends, Scriptures, nature, pastor, employer, legitimate civil authorities, the Spirit in prayer, others' needs, EVERY INBREAKING OF GOD INTO OUR LIVES.

87
Different "Yeses" to God's Invitations

"I don't want her or him to become a sister, brother, priest. I want grandchildren." "Who's going to be there for me when I'm old?" I have heard these words many times. We cannot envision the future of a person: to realize that the priest or brother or sister will have a "family" of thousands, that many of these ministers will cherish, support, and be there for his or her parents; to discover that the child who became a priest or religious may be the one who is most available in times of crisis. My father had the "grandfather" objection; however, when I was Novice Director for 105 young women, he brought food to the Novitiate for all of them. Later he bragged about positions I held or travels I experienced. Before I entered the Convent, I expected to sleep on a straw mat, never see family again, and fade into oblivion when I stepped across that threshold. To the contrary, those of us who took that step found that we were blessed with a marvelous education, travel opportunities beyond our wildest expectations, the grace of living with ethical holy people, spiritual graces we did not dream of, and challenges to use God's gifts to us.

Vocation is about saying "yes" to using God's gifts for others. For some it is the call to priesthood or religious life; for most it is not. Happiness, serenity, personal growth, integration lie in saying a "yes" to recognizing gifts and using them (stretching them) to bring joy and fulfillment to God's People. I imagine us as a giant Mirror, together reflecting the mystery, magnificence, and majesty of God. If each of us did not answer our special vocations, there would be a section of Mirror not reflected.

Spiritual direction is one ministry the Church utilizes to assist us in knowing gifts and discerning where they can be spent—for personal and spiritual development, and service. Other religious traditions are now preparing spiritual directors to minister to members. It is our heritage; and we have these spiritual companions in our parishes, retreat centers, and spiritual centers—to listen with us to God's Call to match our gifts with the cries of the world's people and Mother Earth.

88
Culpable or Willful Ignorance

In one of my "former lives" I did chemical and microbiological research at Oregon State University. The marriage of Religion and Science is still of high interest to me. I recently received the 2014 Scientific Integrity calendar of the Union of Concerned Scientists who work with religious leaders to preserve human values and the earth we inhabit. The cover shows legislators asking: "And this thing, if it does indeed exist, offers enlightenment, hope, and the potential to unlock the mysteries of the universe to all people? Sounds very powerful and maybe too dangerous to be trusted to the masses. What did you call it again?" And, the person being interrogated responds, "Science, Senator. It's called science."

Too often citizens and leaders, parishioners and church officials, make decisions without studying facts, without getting our hands dirty—making un-informed and hurtful decisions that affect "the masses." Pope Francis walked among those masses to know what it feels like to be destitute. So did Archbishop Romero, Gandhi, Mandela, and many religious and government leaders who worked for justice, jobs, health care, and freedom for their people. I recall Archbishop Howard (Archbishop of Portland in Oregon for 40 years and who died at 104) walking from his home, through the city, greeting all his people—poor and wealthy alike—as he strode daily to the Chancery office. These leaders were, in a sense, gathering social and scientific research as a sound basis for making moral decisions.

In Moral Theology Courses we learned about Culpable or Willful Ignorance, the "should have known better" ignorance that resulted from our not being interested enough to do this kind of personal and scientific research. We were culpably ignorant—guilty for making ill-formed or immoral decisions that affected adversely the lives of our sisters and brothers. It is imperative that we do our own research to get the facts on the issues that face us in today's world; we need to walk among and work with those whom we call the "have nots" on the streets. We can encourage each other to write to persuade Leaders in Congress to move among their people who are hungry, homeless, lacking in health care; and urge them to listen to the concerned scientists who invest their lives trying to improve human life and to preserve a healthy planet for all of us.

89
Catholic Social Teachings

Catholic Social Teachings are a rich treasure of wisdom about building a just society and living lives of holiness amidst the challenges of human family. This preamble by the United States Conference of Catholic Bishops precedes their summary of those teachings. Each month we might take the opportunity to reflect on and live in depth one of those teachings. Briefly they are:

- LIFE AND DIGNITY OF THE HUMAN PERSON:
  Human life is sacred, and the dignity of the human person is the foundation of a moral vision for society.
- CALL TO FAMILY, COMMUNITY, AND PARTICIPATION:
  Human beings are social, and how we organize society—in family life, church structures, economics, politics, law, policy—directly affects human dignity and the capacity of persons to grow in community.
- RIGHTS AND RESPONSIBILITIES: Every person has a fundamental right to life and a right to what is required for human decency; corresponding to these rights are responsibilities to each other, families, and society.
- OPTION FOR THE POOR AND VULNERABLE: Our moral test, and fidelity to the Gospel, is the way we care for the most vulnerable members of the human family.

- THE DIGNITY OF WORK AND RIGHTS OF WORKERS: Work is more than a way to make a living; it is a form of continuing participation in God's creation.
- SOLIDARITY: We are one human family, whatever our national, racial, ethnic, economic, and ideological differences; we are our brothers' and sisters' keepers; loving our neighbors has global dimensions in a shrinking world.
- CARE FOR GOD'S CREATION: We show our respect for our Creator by our stewardship of creation; the environmental challenge has moral and ethical dimensions and is a vital element of our Faith as Catholic Christians.

I have learned that other people are also interested in learning about and living these values.

90
Mary Sign of Hope for God's People Today

MARY'S PLACE IN THE CHURCH

September 12 is the Feast of the Holy Name of Mary, a woman Catholics and other Christians consider to be a human being significant to all Christian history. Often, however, Protestants are puzzled by our recognition of the significance of Mary, dedication of places to Our Lady, devotions to the Blessed Virgin as Mother of Jesus. A deep reverence for Mary has become part of Catholic Christian culture: think of Our Lady of Lourdes, Our Lady of Fatima; mysteries of the Rosary; medals to recall her as intercessor; the patronage of the Immaculate Conception. This confusion on the part of Protestants has led some persons to conclude that Catholics "worship" Mary in these symbolic expressions of her extraordinary worth in the sight of God.

Fathers of Vatican Council II chose not to write a separate document on Mary. Instead they placed her within the Dogmatic Constitution on the Church *(Lumen Gentium).* It opens with familiar words, "He for us, and our salvation, came down from heaven, and was incarnated by the Holy Spirit from the Virgin Mary." Mary was given a mission: "the union of the mother and the Son in the work of salvation is made manifest from the time of Christ's virginal conception up to his death." She is invoked by the Catholic Church as Advocate, Helper, Benefactor, and Mediatrix.

"This, however, is so understood that it neither takes away anything from nor adds anything to the dignity and efficacy of Christ the one Mediator...No creature could ever be counted along with the Incarnate Word and Redeemer..." Mary was gifted with Divine Motherhood, but she was always one of us.

TRULY OUR SISTER

Theologian Elizabeth Johnson's book on Mary is titled, *Truly Our Sister*. Mary is a young woman who was born in an unimportant place, walked dusty roads, cooked meals, cared for her Child, welcomed neighbors, and lived as a devout Jew. Like us, she did not fully understand God's Plan, though she asked intelligent questions. She traveled to Bethlehem, Egypt, the foot of the Cross. She continues to walk with us, as together we make our human choices to participate in the Redeemer's Plan for the Salvation of humankind.

91
Church's Heritage of Spiritual Guides

After a session with my Spiritual Director recently, I thought it may be beneficial to reflect during this Christian Unity Week on our heritage of spiritual guides among us—since the time of Saints Peter and Paul. Think of Mary gathering villagers in her home, Jesus meeting others in synagogue, Paul sharing the Good News in person and in letters; then there were the Fathers and Mothers of the Desert, in Medieval Times the Benedicts and Hildegards, in the Sixteen Century Theresa of Avila and Ignatius of Loyola. From the first century to the present, God has provided persons who can journey with us during our spiritual lives: listening to ways our Loving God is with us in prayer, liturgy, family life, work, friendships, joys, sufferings—every moment of our lives.

A spiritual guide-director listens with heart and mind, questioning and affirming us, and discerning with us ways we can integrate our complex lives to achieve a sense of centeredness and wholeness. She or he does not "tell us what to do" but listens to us, to the Spirit alive in us, and to her or his own inner voice. They keep us honest! And committed to growth in the spiritual life, parallel to our growth professionally, socially, intellectually, psychologically, culturally, and theologically! Whereas we might pay psychiatrists $125 to $300 an hour, Spiritual Directors negotiate a sliding scale, so it is affordable to everyone (usually any fee between $5 and $100 an hour) to make this spiritual practice affordable to everyone.

Though women and men, lay and cleric have engaged in the Church's mission of Spiritual Direction for centuries, a few decades ago we expected the priest or minister (we had 2-5 priests in some parishes) to do all the individual Spiritual Direction and we tended to "mix" notions of reconciliation in the Sacrament of Penance with the ongoing spiritual growth that takes place in Spiritual Direction. Now our priests pastor several parishes or administer both a Church and School; they simply do not have time to do ongoing individual or group Spiritual Direction.

Instead, not only parishes but also retreat houses and spiritual centers—e.g. Shalom, Mt. Angel, Our Lady of Peace, Namaste, Loyola, Interfaith Spiritual Center in Oregon (every state has spiritual centers)—have women and men, lay and religious, spiritual directors. Many Christians are re-claiming this practice, one element of the richness of our Judeo-Christian Heritage.

OCTOBER

92
Nurturing the Introverted Child for the Power of Leadership

Though we cannot make the claim, 2000 years later, that Jesus was an introvert, he manifested many of the qualities we now attribute to that personality style: ability to listen to people, skills at drawing people with a diversity of gifts to His enterprise of forwarding the Reign of God, eagerness to heal the wounded, sensitivity to rich and poor, awareness of the lilies of the field, care to think and pray before He acted. These gifts are seldom applauded in our extroverted "Culture of Personality" in which the general public and business schools are told: "If you don't have all the facts—and usually you don't—speak and act anyway; if you hesitate, you risk losing others' trust." Or: "The person who speaks first, sets the agenda."

Our introverted and very gifted children (and potential parish and civic leaders) are too often bullied, personally or on the web—we have read the tragic results! So much so that numerous articles like "How to Raise-Encourage an Introverted Child" are being written. Another resource, *Quiet: The Power of Introverts in a World That Can't Stop Talking* (Susan Cain) is a good choice for parents, teachers, and all who facilitate for young people the best use of God-given talents.

We don't want our children to become Tony Roberts; nor to hear of him or her, "No thought ever went unspoken." We can suggest reading about inspiring introverts: Gandhi, Rosa Parks,

T.S. Eliot, Steve Wozniak, Eleanor Roosevelt, Bill Gates, to name a few—persons who developed innate gifts and interests like those of the introverted child.

We can discover ways to facilitate our children's introvert gifts for study, compassion, and concern for and service to the world beyond themselves. For example, the "nerd" could offer the bully some help with math (in this case he-she is in power). The introverted student can write convincing articles in the paper. He or she can take notes at meetings, and report back, assuring that every voice is heard. Writing scripts for school plays could bring their "voices" forward. She or he can offer to chair a meeting, and ascertain that all are recognized. The artist can "say" a lot too!

The world needs extroverts like Bill Clinton and Franklin Roosevelt, but, as Anais Nin says, "Our culture .... Lost our center and we have to find it again."

93
Three Thank-You's a Day

"Ten were cleansed. Where are the other nine?" Jesus asked. When we were novices, our Gregorian Chant Professor shared this pearl of Wisdom that I have cherished to this day: "If every day you thank God for three things, you will never become a bitter person." I can hear her soft voice in my heart through every disappointment and failure. When I drive through Portland the red and orange and yellow splashes of Autumn leaves remind me of my pledge! Others too must have discovered a lifelong call to live an Attitude of Gratitude.

Sarah Ban Breathnach wrote *The Simple Abundance Journal of Gratitude*, allowing the reader-participant to write five things each day for which she or he is grateful. In the foreword she reflects: "Gratitude holds us together even as we're falling apart. Ironically, gratitude's most powerful mysteries are often revealed when we stumble in the darkness, rage in anger, hurl faith across the room, abandon all hope. While we cry ourselves to sleep, gratitude waits patiently to console and reassure us; there is a landscape larger than the one we see." It's quite easy to fill this journal in a year with the good things God sends us daily.

On YouTube the story of Pastor Nicholas James Vujicic, *"No arms no legs no worries,"* demonstrates an unlimited landscape. Watch it for a lift and to re-commit oneself to an Attitude of Gratitude. Born in Australia without arms or legs, he was tempted to commit suicide at age eight. Yet, he is an inspirational speaker, illustrating, that with God's blessing one can "live without limits." He swims, boats, does "stand-up" comedy. Nick loves to "freak people out" and to talk about bullying. He calls himself Prince Charming with a couple of pieces missing. Now married to Kanae Miyahera, he is a father, a pastor, a speaker, a delightful whole person.

With our government seemingly frozen in the decision-making process, the world's nations at war for the rights they believe they deserve, people feeling that they don't get their "fair share of life," it could be easy to join the nine cured lepers who did not return to say "thank you." How much better to be alongside the one who said "Thank you" to Jesus. As one company puts it: "Life's Good."

94
Steadying Another's Hands

As long as Aaron and Hur supported Moses' hands, they remained steady, and Israel was victorious. In the beginning God had said, "It is not good for humans to be alone." Later, Jesus called men and women to be at His side as disciples, preaching, healing, leading. Throughout the Hebrew Bible-Old Testament-First Testament and the Christian Bible-New Testament-Second Testament, we are reminded that we are social beings, God's Family, meant to be a caring human community, to offer our unique gifts for the common good of our families, neighbors—and the entire human community.

Perhaps the more we learn, through news media and internet, about wars, divisions, and leanings toward win-lose political situations, the more we become aware of the costs of setting aside our own preferences to support and to "steady another's hands" in their human efforts to succeed. Negotiations, consensus-building, collaboration, discernment until the group reaches a common goal or mission are community challenges which we encounter weekly at work, at home, in a parish, and at political gatherings.

Pope Francis, in the America Magazine Interview, mentioned the word "discernment" a number of times. Discernment requires that we put our own ideas and preferences on the shelf for a while, that we listen prayerfully to the quiet inner voice of the Holy Spirit telling us what might be best for all, that we attend carefully to what others are hearing and speaking as a result of their prayer and experiences, that we speak our own truth with a certain level of spiritual detachment, that together we "hold each other" in seeking God's Wisdom, Goodness, Beauty—and the values that promote human dignity.

Not a week passes but that we are faced with family, parish, and work decisions about car payments, tuition, rising grocery bills, stretching time to meet commitments, balancing priorities, the price of gas or new tennis shoes for the children's sports activities. With the onset of cold nights, we add our concerns for the growing number of homeless in our cities. Possibly we have reached an era of awareness and sensitivity greater than at any time in human history—along with the invitation to "hold each other's hands steady" so that each of us can be more successful in the "Mission of Living Successful and Satisfying Human Lives."

95
Interpretations Can Unite or Divide

A FIVE HUNDRED YEAR DIVISION

Human interpretation of the book of Galatians led Christians to 500 years (1517-1999) of division between Lutherans and Roman Catholics. How is Galatians to be interpreted? Is one saved by Faith alone, or by Faith and Good Works? Interpretations of what we read or hear can divide or unite spouses, friends, congregations, and Faith Traditions.

The document on a common understanding of justification (October 31, 1999) reads:

> *Lutheran churches and the Roman Catholic Church have together listened since 1964 to the good news proclaimed in Holy Scripture. This common listening, together with theological conversations of recent years, has led to a shared understanding of justification. This encompasses a consensus in basic truths; differing explications in particular statements are compatible with it.*
>
> *In faith we together hold the conviction that justification is the work of the triune God. The Father sent his Son into the world to save sinners. The foundation and presupposition of justification is the incarnation, death, and resurrection of Christ. Justification means that Christ himself is our righteousness, in which we share through the Holy Spirit in accord with the will of the*

Father. Together we confess: By grace alone, in faith in Christ's saving work and not because of any merit on our part, we are accepted by God and receive the Holy Spirit, who renews our hearts while equipping and calling us to good works.

FACTS AND PRAYER BEFORE INTERPRETATION

If interpretation of realities can divide persons and religions, maybe we need to look at ways we interpret daily what we see and hear. Do we get the facts and pray about issues before we judge or speak harshly? Or, do we look at one leg of the elephant to describe it? Do we interpret a cluster of laughing persons as focusing on us? Do we interpret someone's tardiness as a "don't care attitude" instead of wondering if she had to care for a sick parent? Do we interpret a political figure as "bad" because we disagree with one of his or her positions? Perhaps we can do a better job at interpreting, from an informed intellect and a compassionate heart, what we see, hear, read, —a step toward union with others, not divisions of 500 years!

96
Compassionate God

"Without any doubt people today suffer and vegetate in isolation; they need a superior impulse to intervene and force them to pass beyond the level at which they are immobilized, leading them to discover their profound affinities. The sense of Earth is the irresistible pressure which will come at the right moment to unite them in a common passion." (Teilhard De Chardin)

"I am compassionate," God says, in Exodus, after spelling out for the people how they are to treat the aliens, orphans, widows, poor neighbors, and the person without a cloak to cover his body at sunset. Jesus reiterates (and adds to) God's message in Deuteronomy, expressed in Matthew as: "You shall love the Lord, your God, with all your heart, with all your soul, and with all your mind. This is the greatest and first commandment. The second is like it: You shall love your neighbor as yourself."

Our Buddhist sisters and brothers also ask us to practice lovingkindness and compassion. In fact, if we look at the primary principles guiding all the world's religions, from ancient Confucianism to newly founded ones, their scriptures or writings capture the essences in two words, LOVE and COMPASSION.

Sometimes it takes world crises to jolt us into "putting flesh" on the most important values in human history and giving up our "me first" or "not in my backyard" individualism to act together as a human family to cure our ills. It occurred to me that the Ebola Crisis and the ISIS Crisis and mass shootings could be graces for all of us in every nation. One shooter can kill dozens of human beings in minutes, and one deadly organism has the potential for destroying all of humankind!

Maybe one word of Love or one act of Compassion—from each of us—toward somebody in our family (with whom we have not been reconciled), work setting (who seems to be depressed or fearful of losing a job), person on the street (who has no cloak or sleeping bag for after sunset), government leader (whose values do not harmonize with mine), Church official (whom we may be tempted to ask that he practice what he preaches)—could eventually bring healing to the people of the earth. Television and all of our wonderful technological tools and media let us know almost immediately about the sufferings among all nations. We have within our power to use our human talents and technology to heal many of the miseries we witness—but it takes our heads, hands, and HEARTS OF LOVE AND COMPASSION to heal a world that is way too big a task for any one nation.

97
Faithfulness

When we children were sitting at my English Grandfather's feet, near his yukky spittoon, listening to stories from the "olden times"—e.g. about one of my relatives, Maime, who took a train to Congress to lobby for benefits for Civil War Veterans (she finally won!)—Faithfulness was not in my vocabulary. However, Faithfulness was in my early life experience. Will, my Grandfather, an Anglican, had married Esther, a Roman Catholic and an herbalist; together they raised 13 (yes, thirteen) healthy children; she still kissed Will (and all guests) warmly and fed them home-made bread and pie, and each day he discussed life with her over tea at a table graced with a lace tablecloth.

In my entire lifetime I have witnessed Faithfulness in myriad ways. Every October Sisters of the Holy Names of Jesus and Mary who made vows 60, 70, or 75 years ago, renew their vows and celebrate with their community, family, and friends. At times I add up the total number of years (hundreds) during which they served the People of God with a loving Faithfulness—and most of these Sisters still continue to minister.

Decades of Faithfulness seem like a miracle in a culture of individualism, rapid change, re-location of families to all parts of the world, education that moves couples and friends in many different directions, exposure to material attractions, little time for reflection and prayer and studies of spiritual values, a wide range of values among family members and generations—many forces which could polarize us or pull us to opposite ends of a magnet. Yet, we are even now touched by articles about married couples who have been together for 50, 60, 70, and even 80 years!

When I was a novice I memorized St. Paul's letter to the Corinthians, the part which speaks about the virtues remaining for all eternity — now, that's Faithfulness — these three remain, Faith, Hope, and Charity, and the greatest of these is Charity."

Marshal B. Rosenberg, PhD, in his *Nonviolent Communication*, offers four steps (express observations, feelings, needs, requests) toward a language for life and Faithfulness of a shared life for 17 (a real number), 25, 50, or more years. It's a model we may wish to consider!

98

The Lord Hears the Cry of the Poor

Sirach assures us that God hears the cry of the oppressed. "The prayer of the lowly pierces the clouds; it does not rest till it reaches its goal, nor will it withdraw till the Most High responds, judges justly and affirms the right..." Sirach [Hebrew] or Ecclesiasticus [Latin] is what we call a Wisdom Book in the Writings section of the Bible. These books address the human condition, using concrete symbols and down-to-earth terms that appeal to Jews, Christians, and even those who do not embrace the Bible as their Scriptures. The Psalm response, "The Lord Hears the Cry of the Poor," is repeated often during liturgies throughout the year.

Sirach and the Wisdom writers need to be heard at this time in history! Zygmunt Bauman, a wise professor emeritus at the University of Leeds, and one of the world's leading social thinkers for decades, questions, "Does the richness of the few benefit us all?" While the richest 1 percent of adults in the world own 40 percent of global assets, and the richest 10 percent account for 85 percent of the total wealth of the world, the bottom half of the world's adult population owns 1 percent of global wealth. This is a "crisis" question. Bauman offers the reflection which tugs at our hearts as well, as we try to live and teach the messages of the Hebrew Bible - Old Testament - First Testament, and the Christian Bible - New Testament - Second Testament: *"The stubborn persistence of poverty on a planet in the throes of economic growth fundamentalism is enough to make thoughtful people pause and reflect on the direct as much as the collateral casualties of that redistribution of wealth. The deepening abyss separating the poor and prospectless from the well-off, sanguine, self-confident and boisterous is an obvious reason to be gravely concerned."*

Maybe this reality is a call to reflection and prayer: For whom do I vote? Do I write to my Senators and Representatives? Where do I shop? What resources do I really need? How can I share with others who have less than I? The problem is gigantic and global: How can Catholics, other Christians, Jews, and those of many Traditions make a difference—hear the voices of the poor, and help make their voices heard by those who can bring about distribution of wealth?

99
Community Spirituality

Jesus Gathered an Evangelizing Community

Jesus gathered fishermen, tax collectors, and women like Mary Magdalene to be His evangelizing community. He not only invited them to the intimacy of community, to "Come and see where He lived," but He also sent them out with the words, "Go and make disciples of all nations." Jerry C. Doherty, Rector of Church of the Ascension in Stillwater, Minnesota, names "Three American Crises" in his book *A Celtic Model of Ministry, the Reawakening of Community Spirituality.*

- Crisis of Individualism. Countered by Community.
- Crisis of Faith. Filled by Mysticism.
- Crisis of Lifestyle. Resolved by a Gospel Way of Life.

A Welcoming Community Reaches Out

Sometimes we need "stickers on our assignments" to recognize we're listening to the Spirit and learning to "do life right." Under the leadership of pastor, staff, council, and commission leaders, reawakenings are happening:

- Small Community groups gather for prayer and support, but also to serve God's People: Liturgy, Altar Servers and Sacristans, Hospitality, Vocations, Rose Gardens, Book Club, Cub and Boy Scouts, Knights of Columbus, Soup with Friends, Care for the Planet, Blanchet House, Peace and Justice, Sanctity of Life, St. Vincent de Paul, Grief and Bereavement, Stay-at-Home Moms, Parents of Mentally Ill Children, Men's Group, Others.

- Our Mystical hearts are being fed by Weekend and Daily Liturgies, Children's Liturgy, Contemplative Prayer, Individual and Group Spiritual Direction, Faith-Sharing, RCIA, Biblical Studies, Reconciliation, Eucharist to the Homebound, the daily strength of praying for and with others.
- An extra buttress to living Gospel hopes and dreams for ourselves and our world comes with living daily the Paschal Mystery; reading Lectio Divina; and listening (as we walk or drive) to Christmas or Easter CDs.

It's a big temptation to "do roasts" on ourselves. But a little confidence in the richness of what we are being and doing goes a long way toward encouraging generosity to give blessings away, to make real the call extended to us—empowered by a Loving Community.

100
From Mustard Seed to World Harvest

"Fall, season of Harvest." The seeds have developed and borne fruit, and the pumpkin patch is waiting for the children to visit. Jesus calls us, in season and out of season, to plant the seeds of Faith: "Go out to all the world…" Scripture and Catholic Social Teachings plant energy and life under our mustard seeds of faith wherever we go in this "wide, wide world."

Wherever we "live and move and have our being" the world seems to be getting smaller. That's both bad news and good news. People struggle to communicate better, make decisions that affect many lives, work toward consensus for what they believe to be the common good: Republicans and Democrats in the USA, Syrian leaders and people, African rebels and authorities, people all over the wide world. Financial, political, religious, and cultural crises impact not only entire nations but every other nation as well. And yet, when countries suffer an earthquake, flood, or tsunami, other countries know of it almost immediately and can and do offer assistance. Families can contact each other in minutes via Skype or telephone, 911 calls save lives, and PGE keeps customers abreast of downed power lines during terrible storms.

I often reflect on the lives of Jesus, Mary, and Joseph living in an insignificant village called Nazareth, doing simple things like cooking, planting gardens, building furniture, going to temple—never traveling to Europe or North America. Yet their love, hospitality, prayer, and celebration of life have made more difference to our wide world than has any other "important person" from a significant place like New York, Paris, or London. Pablo Casalis reminds us of our potential impact in planting our unique mustard seeds: "It takes courage for people to listen to their own goodness and to act on it."

101
Jesus Called Laborers for the Harvest

My three brothers, "Navy Men," chided me, "Not just in the Navy. Join the Convent and see the world"! I am often humbled by the reality that I, "the nun," was given many advantages that my two sisters have not had. Though it is true that my work in the Congregation has sent me to places in the U.S.A., Canada, Mexico, Peru, Jerusalem, Turkey, Vietnam, England, Ireland, France, Germany, Italy, and other sites; allowed me to receive the best of educations; hear glorious music; make spiritual retreats; receive the words of wise lecturers; study the Bible; and read literature from Aristotle to Rahner—that's not the best part of being called by Jesus to be a full-time laborer in God's fields. The best part is being "sent in God's Name."

Jesus sent seventy-two, in pairs, to be laborers in the harvest. Now, the fields needing a "yes" answer of a Carmelite nun, Trappist monk, lay minister, brother, sister, deacon, priest, minister, and others committed to lifetime work in that harvest seem only to have widened since Jesus' time. People ask me how one figures out whether she or he—or a child or friend—has such a call-vocation, since God works through ordinary human events and real people. I've noticed some indications to consider in prayer: Do I tend to "see God in all things" or am I attracted to frequent prayer or participation in Mass? Is there a group of persons whom I could serve well, with my particular gifts—youth, the elderly, the sick, addicts, young people who are intellectuals? Am I already living, or am I drawn to live, a simple lifestyle, a commitment to celibacy for the sake of God's harvest, a readiness to listen to and respond to the needs across my world? Do I exhibit a pattern of keeping commitments, even when it's tough? Do I enjoy the beauties of life, the goodness of an informed conscience, and the search for Wisdom and Truth? Is there some kind of a "mysterious nudge" within me, inviting me to discern with a spiritual director, priest, brother, sister, deacon, lay minister, wise lay person?

Maybe many more of us are invited to accept Jesus' invitation and say "Yes" because "The Laborers are too few..."

NOVEMBER

102
Why Do Catholics Honor Saints?

When we enter a Catholic or Orthodox home we notice icons, statues, pictures of saints displayed. At one time babies were named for the saint on whose feast day they were born: March 17, St. Patrick's Day, became the name day for many Patricks and Patricias; and many a Francis or Frances was born on October 4 named after St. Francis of Assisi. When we need to find lost articles, we ask for the help of St. Anthony; and when money runs short we appeal to St. Joseph. I can still see the angel in my Grandmother's guest bedroom hovering over two children attempting to cross a rickety bridge.

We celebrate the Feast of All Saints and the Commemoration of All the Faithful Departed. We highlight in the Liturgies one of the major doctrines of the Catholic Faith since the fifth century: the Communion of Saints, the belief that all of us on earth and in heaven, as well as the angels, are "connected" in the Holy Spirit in a significant way. At our Liturgies, we pray, often antiphonally, the Contemporary Litany of the Saints.

Though Catholics and Orthodox are accused of offering "worship" to saints whom they honor and venerate, they are actually recognizing members in the Communion of Saints who loved and served God with extraordinary affection. Early in church history, saints were primarily martyrs. Since then we emulate holy people because, despite their limits and faults, they exhibited great love toward their God and human beings who needed their help.

Because, like Jesus, we are incarnate beings, we venerate the saints in a number of concrete, tangible ways: icons, statues, pictures in our homes or on our dashboards; stained glass windows in our churches named for St. Luke or St. Matthew or St. Agnes or St. Cosmos; offering a nine-day novena asking St. Francis Xavier to keep our missions vital for God's People; or taking a relic of a saint known for his or her healing powers to a sick friend.

In a world becoming more and more secularized, lonely, and alienated from family and friends, we need to be assured that there are "holy presences" to whom we are intimately and forever attached, in the Communion of Saints.

103
A Great Sadness?

When I was young I read a quote that "stuck" all of my life: "There is but one sadness, and it is that we are not all saints." (Leon Bloy) All of us are expected to be saints? Saints Peter and Paul make sainthood seem possible. Ordinary vocation: Peter was a fisherman. Ordinary irritations: Paul speaks of a "thorn in the flesh" that would not go away. Yet each of them loved Jesus and served God's People ...and died doing so.

Recently Pope Francis canonized Pope John XXIII and Pope John Paul II. But he had also recognized and gave to us other models of sanctity: hundreds of 15th century un-named martyrs who were beheaded for refusing to convert to Islam; 813 Italian martyrs of Otranto who were slain in 1480 for defying demands of Turkish invaders, a 20th century Columbian nun who worked as teacher and spiritual guide to indigenous people, and Mexican Maria Guadalupe Garcia Zavala, who nursed the sick and helped people during the persecution by the government in the 1920s. The beauty and consolation of all of these saints is this: they come from every country, representing every culture, gender, age. Maybe it is possible for all of us to be saints, after all!

We know of some of the foibles of Peter, Paul, Pope John XXIII, Pope John Paul II. Yet they "made it," they discovered what the call to true evangelization means: to live to the best of their ability a life like that of Christ, to give everything they could to the service of others, to express their unique charisms (gifts) during their lifetimes.

We need saints! We can ask them to help us heal, to forgive, to serve those who are not attractive to us, to enjoy life (Philip Neri), to keep Faith and Hope when we feel discouraged, to use our gifts instead of holding back, to assist us as we puzzle over the truths of our Faith (Thomas Aquinas), to be political in loving and intelligent ways (Thomas More), to care for the under-served (Elizabeth Seton). Truly there is but one sadness, that we are not all saints (with all our warts and wonders). Maybe we could cure the world of violence and greed.

104
Legacy

My mother, Elizabeth LaVina (Betty), asked me often, when I visited her at Mother Joseph's Care Center in Olympia, "Why doesn't God come for me?" I would answer, "I guess God doesn't have the room ready yet, Mama." This brought a smile, the kind they found on her lips when they found her on Palm Sunday—because she told God she wanted to be in heaven for Easter!

All of us saints in the Body of Christ leave Legacies. Our Jewish foremothers and forefathers, as did old Isaac, called their children to their bedsides and shared the Wisdom that was the Heritage they wished to pass on. We call that Legacy an Ethical Will or a Wisdom Will. Each of us leaves a Legacy: ways that we modeled a compassionate heart, a listening ear, a helping hand with a burden that another carried; the healing that happened when we forgave wrongs; the prayerful support when a friend lost a loved one, the financial assistance we contributed when a job flew out the window unexpectedly.

Some people now write out a Wisdom Will for children and grandchildren, often in the form of a letter to loved ones. They write out dreams, visions, hopes, blessings that they would wish for them, and ask that copies be shared at the time of their deaths.

The Wisdom Will letter is not only a practice that is a Treasure for survivors; it is also a priceless gift to oneself. We notice, flowing out of our very fingers, some gifts and talents and values that God has bequeathed to us. And, we recall the quote, "The one to whom much has been given, much will be asked." We are moved to bestow at least some of our heritage now, on living members of the Communion of Saints.

The Communion of Saints has always been a meaningful Catholic doctrine for me and others. My Mother, your departed loved ones, your family, the grandfather by whose bed you pray as he takes his final journey back to the Creator's arms, friends living and dead—all of us are intimately connected in some Mysterious Way. The Book of Wisdom says that "the Faithful will abide in God in Love"—and we can add, on Earth as it is in Heaven!

105
Our Still Point in Our Fast-Changing World

As theologians we study translated clay tablets from Ancient Near East, parchment scrolls from Egypt, and books from every nation. Former scholars of Biblical studies, theology, philosophy, psychology, and many disciplines find themselves with a life-time collection of BOOKS. Often, we grieve as we give away books; authors have become our "friends" with whom we dialogued and taught their ideas. I received permission of superiors to keep books until I was no longer a university or seminary professor. When I moved to a CCRC (continuous care retirement community), I gave away 26 boxes to Powell's, 16 to Marylhurst University (I had previously given 100s of books to them), 8 boxes to a Russian Orthodox community, and dozens to friends. However, many if not most of us, no longer read clay tablets, parchment scrolls, or even—books. Truly the computer, iPad, tablet, iBook, and other technological developments have shifted dramatically the ways we access information!

The "wheels of life" travel rapidly in our fast-changing world. This acceleration of change is experienced by most people in our world. Perhaps Pope Francis' appeal to have the elderly and young take time to dialogue will fill in the connections of past, present, and hopes for the future. I plan to facilitate an intergenerational retreat for just that purpose.

I am hearing young people, as well as those who grew up in the "book world" instead of the "tech world" express the desire for solitude, time in the woods, moments to gaze at the Autumn leaves. Time to Be Still and find their Sacred Center. Every Ford or Mercedes tire that moves across the freeway at 70 miles per hour turns smoothly because the axel is secure. We need a secure axel —A STILL POINT— a Center that allows us to stay integrated as we move all-to-quickly from commitment to commitment, as we experience the rapidity of change.

We believe in the Indwelling Trinity—Creator that holds entire solar systems in place, Redeemer who changed our world irreversibly, Spirit that moves us moment-by-moment toward realization of personal gifts to be offered for all people. We can pause at our computers, take a deep breath as we walk to the next room, appeal for Wisdom as we turn the car key, hum a thanksgiving as we rock a baby.

Our Still Point, a God who is our Trinitarian "axel," keeps us secure as we move with the wheels of today's world.

106
Promises Kept

Companies seem to believe that we need to hear commercials more than 70 times 7 to have them "register" in the human consciousness. I wonder if the Wise God knew that phenomenon long ago! The Hebrew Biblical authors told God's People over and over and over that God would send the Messiah, that a Child would be born in Bethlehem, that Persons from the East would follow a star. Advent Preparation has been a Reality for centuries!

We pray with the Advent Candle during four weeks of preparation, and open a calendar for each day, with a Scripture passage for our reflection. People all over the world engage in meaningful practices to ready themselves for the coming of Jesus. Peru has a lovely Advent practice: a "pocket calendar." Children and adults can find in each pocket a special quote or gift during Advent; one can also put a personal gift in each pocket daily (e.g. some transformation we wish to make in our own lives). We can learn much about a country or a religion by reading about their Advent Preparations for the Coming of Jesus the Christ.

Besides the external practices, some daily reflections deepen our awareness of the fullness of this Season.

- The first week, for example, we can reflect on Hope (Jeremiah 33:14; Luke 21:26-27). We have seen the social fabric of our world unravel; yet, hope comes only when hope seems gone.

- The second week, on Repentance (Baruch 5:1; Luke 3:3). Perfection in life is not possible; we are tied to God by a thread, and sometimes we break the cord and need to have it re-tied.
- The third week, on Contentment (Zephaniah 3:17; Luke 3:10-14). True contentment, as Chesterton says, is "the power of getting out of any situation all that there is in it."
- The fourth week, on Commitment (Micah 5:2; Luke 1:45). We live in a society where many people go hungry, where boys and girls and women and men are trafficked for the use of the greedy. Commitment means we do something that makes life better for others, no matter how small and inept we feel.
- Christmas day (Isaiah 52:9; John 1:12-13). This day is the culmination of Advent, and sends us on the road to new life, new awareness, and a new energy to be an incarnate presence of God for others.

107
Attitude of Gratitude

At least 30 of the 150 Psalms in the Hebrew Bible are prayers of Thanksgiving. Praying these Psalms regularly helps us shape a grateful and loving heart. Jesus the Jew Himself prayed the Psalms daily, as do many lay persons, sisters, brothers, and priests. We refer to the compilation of these 150 psalms and accompanying prayers as The Breviary or Book of Christian Prayer. *Laudate* and *iBreviary* are free on the Web now!

As I mentioned, I have treasured a little book, *The Simple Abundance Journal of Gratitude*, by Sarah Ban Breathnach. Her cornucopia of words spill out the benefits of Gratitude:

> "*Gratitude is the most passionate transformative force in the cosmos. When we offer thanks to God or to another human being, gratitude gifts us with renewal, reflection, reconnection. Gratitude bestows reverence, allowing us to encounter everyday epiphanies, those transcendent moments of awe that change forever how we experience life and the world. Once we accept that abundance and lack are parallel realities and that each day we choose—consciously or unconsciously—which world we will inhabit, a deep inner shift in our reality occurs. We discover the sacred in the ordinary and we realize that every day is literally a gift. How we conduct our daily round, how we celebrate it, cherish it and consecrate it*

is how we express our thankfulness to the Giver of all good."

Three practices come to me that may be blessings for our families during this season of Thanksgiving and Advent: (1) At our Thanksgiving Dinner, each person mentions one way that God has gifted our Country, Family, or Individual Person; (2) For 30 days, from today until Christmas Day, write 5 overlooked blessings that you personally encounter each day (a sunset? the aroma of turkey? time for a warm scented bath? an hour in a bookstore? a walk on the beach? breakfast in bed? meeting a kindred spirit? serenity after paying the bills? If you are counting, that makes 150 overlooked blessings!); (3) Pray one of the Psalms of Gratitude each day. (According to some scholars they are Psalms 8, 18, 19, 29, 30, 32, 33, 34, 36, 40, 41, 66, 103, 104, 105, 106, 111, 113, 116, 117, 125, 133, 135, 136, 138, 139, 146, 147, 148, 150).

Most especially we thank our Provident God for the Gift of Life!

108
Zeal for God's Temple

I am amazed at the things I took for granted during my lifetime! I never gave it a thought that God gave me the energy to run down one rail of the local train track, hear the ski instructor say, "Are you a rubber ball or something," teach a whole public school—yep, boys as well as girls—how to dance during the lunch hour (one wife told me later that I had saved her marriage!), and work my way through school from 3rd grade through grad school. Now, at this stage of my life, I thank God for every step I am able to take!

We seldom realize that EVERYTHING IS GIFT and we live somewhat "un-mindfully." Most of us certainly take for granted St. Paul's message in the 1 Corinthians reading: "You are God's building... temples of God... and a Wise Builder laid the foundation..." We call this Presence in us the Indwelling of the Trinity. Our friends from Eastern traditions bow reverently and speak the word *Namaste*, "The God in me recognizes the God in you."

How many times we recall that our children and students asked us questions, and we found our mouths opening and offering responses that really made sense. We were tempted to look over our shoulders to see the Holy Spirit smiling, as we asked, "Where in heaven did that come from?" We actually spoke with Wisdom!

The reality is that we can rely 24/7 on this Indwelling Presence in the Temple built by God in our very beings. We Catholics call this around the clock attention to the Spirit of Wisdom "Awareness." Our Buddhist friends refer to this kind of attending, in all that we do, "Mindfulness."

The spiritual practice of approaching every activity—from cooking pasta to praying—with attention, reverence, and wonder not only helps us become deeper, more reflective, wiser, interesting people, but it also improves our memories, calms our physical well-being (instead of living with stress), and facilitates spiritual integration. Perhaps at least once a day we could recall St. Paul's words, "For the temple of God, which you are, is holy." And, not take this ever-available, marvelous, mysterious Gift for granted.

109
The "Have's" and the "Have Not's"

During many decades of living, I have observed that the "Have Not's" are often immensely thankful for so very little. They model what it means to live with a Grateful Heart. Thanksgiving may be a time to meditate on their lessons.

I recall a day when I was alone, "cruising the warehouses" in Seattle, seeking bargains on sheets and towels for the Convent. A beautiful woman, a prostitute, came up to me and asked, "Could I hold you for just a few minutes?" After our gentle and lingering embrace, she whispered softly, "Thank you." I have never gotten over those words of gratitude; I could have been the "have not" and this woman of beauty and extreme poverty been "the nun" with her education and purse with money for linens, and a surplus to share. It is exceedingly painful for the "have nots" to have nothing to give away—except themselves, and sometimes their own bodies.

At one time in our lives people my age had Dads who drove welfare trucks with flour and powdered milk for poor families, brothers and sisters who complained about having home-made bread in their lunches, and Moms who created "Johnny-cakes" out of flour, cornmeal, milk, and the one egg that my mother prayed for (and actually found in the grass). At Thanksgiving time, we think of those times, the gatherings of the first pilgrims and Native Americans, the rationings during World War II—and now, the thousands of people in our world who are making the most of living in camps or tent cities or cardboard boxes. And yet so often, they, like the prostitute in Seattle, murmur a "Thank You" to God and to those who share what they can with them.

That is why we are so blessed, to live in a country where many people can be counted among the "haves" who can gather as communities to worship God in the incredible prayer of Thanksgiving we name Eucharist, prepare and deliver Thanksgiving baskets, sit around a family table to enjoy turkey and pumpkin pie, and find the surplus in our purses to send to the Catholic Relief Services or Doctors Without Borders for people in the Puerto Rico, or down on the streets near Burnside, or in a Shelter, or right next door!

110
In Praise of Women

Who is the most quoted person in history? Answer: "My Mother." How many times have we heard, "My mother used to say..." Even at the wedding feast of Cana Mary's words influenced the servants, "Do whatever He tells you." Her words, and Jesus' miracle which responded to those words, made the feast a success! Jesus listened and watched and learned from Mary, as have the children of all ages, all over the world, listened and watched their own mothers.

The Book of Proverbs closes with a description of the Valiant Woman: her husband's heart goes out to her, she works with loving hands, she reaches out to the poor and needy, and hearers are urged to praise her at the city gates. I have known many adult women ministry students to multi-task as did she: they studied their theology assignments while they stirred the soup and oversaw their children doing homework at the kitchen table. Recall too that "the nuns" (religious sisters) built hospitals for those who were ill, schools for the uneducated, social agencies for the needy, and helped the Irish and Italians and Polish and immigrants from many countries adjust to a new land and find work to sustain their families. Our own Sisters tell stories of rocking a cradle of an orphan with one foot while they mended stockings and listened to spiritual reading. These women built much of the infrastructure of the Church in the United States. I have heard many men say, "Sister Mary ... is responsible for my becoming a doctor or professor or priest."

Admittedly it is a different world than it was when the Valiant Woman of Proverbs was managing home and profession, or the Sisters of fifty years ago who had fewer vocational choices for women (secretary, hair dresser, teacher, nurse, nun, mother) than we do now; yet, they used their talents to build a more humane, educated, and thriving America for us. In this decade, we continue to stand in awe at the ways women innovate, initiate, and use their entrepreneurial skills to respond creatively to the needs of people of our time. Think of the remarkable contributions to science, technology, space research, politics, education, finance, entertainment, and religion they have made. We stand in praise of women!

“Next to God, we are indebted to women, first for life itself; and then for making it worth having.” (C. Nestell Bovee)

111
Universal Call to Holiness

Lumen Gentium (Vatican II Document, the Church) encourages us:

"...all Christians in any state or walk of life are called to the fullness of Christian life and to the perfection of love, and by this holiness a more human manner of life is fostered also in earthly society." I treasure too the words of Apostolicam Actuositatem (Decree, Apostolate of Lay People): "Laity...share in the priestly, prophetical and kingly office of Christ... they endeavor to have the Gospel spirit permeate and improve the temporal order...lay people are called by God to make of their apostolate, through the vigor of their Christian spirit, a leaven in the world."

"Apps" Readily Available to Us

What makes holiness within universal reach, even in this technological age? During the joyous season of Advent many people meditate about 15 minutes a day on the gifts that Creator, Jesus, and Sprit have offered to us: the personal gifts of heart and intellect, creative and mechanical skills that the Creator gave each of us (from those who are iPad savvy to those who sit praying by the bedside of a hospice patient); a God who first loved us (Jn 13:34); the Holy Spirit sent to us to love God with our whole soul, heart, mind, and strength (Mt 12:30); the fruits of the spirit for our sanctification (Gal 5:22); and a compassionate God who knows our strengths and limits and forgives our shortcomings (Mt 6:12).

The "Global" Reach of Holiness

We sing, "We Can Make a Difference." And what are opportunities for making a difference in society—for being a leaven wherever we are? Being holy? If we are age 3 to 33, we can patiently teach pre-1983 relatives and friends computer skills? If we have "wheels," discover who needs transportation to church, doctor, shopping, food bank, or hair appointment? Our Catholic Tradition reminds us that all of us belong to the "Communion of Saints," and who among us does not need the prayerful support of the Saints of all ages? Irish people have a practice called *kything*: sending up prayer for colleagues, friends, family, people the world over—even if the recipients of those Holy Offerings do not know it. We DO make a difference to our world!

DECEMBER

112
The Jesse Tree and Jesus' Spiritual Heritage

This last decade we have noticed a growing interest in "family trees" and tracing one's heritage. Ancestry.com is sought by thousands; the TV program, Finding Your Roots, has become popular. Jesus too had a "family tree." The Jesse Tree sprang up in Medieval Art and spiritual practice as a way of honoring the 42 generations that preceded the Birth of Jesus. This Tree combines Isaiah's prophecy with the gospel account of Matthew about the descent of Jesus from the royal line of David, whose father was Jesse.

> *"And there shall come forth a rod out of the stem of Jesse, and a Branch shall grow out of his roots; and the Spirit of the Lord shall rest upon Him: the spirit of Wisdom and Understanding, the spirit of Counsel and Fortitude, the spirit of Knowledge, and the Fear of the Lord (Is 11:1,2)."*

Examples of Jesse Tree images are found in carvings, manuscripts, stained glass, embroidered vestments, and other art forms. Hanging (on a tree) symbols of events leading up to Jesus' birth has been revived by families in their efforts to "put Christ back into Christmas." During each evening in Advent, a family member places a symbol on the Tree.

Here are some of the 42 events commemorated in Jesus' spiritual heritage, with a symbol:

- Creation, Gen 1:1-31; 2:1-4, globe of the earth
- Abraham and his lineage, Gen 12:1-3; 13:2-18, many stars
- Moses, Ex 2:1-10; 20:1-17, baby in a basket
- Jesse, 1 Sam 16:1-13; Is 11:1,2, shepherd staff
- David, 1 Sam 16:14-23; 17:12-51, slingshot
- Isaiah, Is 6:1-8, tongs and coal
- Zechariah and Elizabeth, Lk 1:68-79, chalkboard with name "John"
- Joseph, Mt 1:18-25, carpentry tools
- Mary, Mt 1:18-25; Lk 1:26-38, crown of stars

Eight days before Christmas, symbols of the O Antiphons—

- O Wisdom, Sirach 24:2; Wisdom 8:1, open book
- O Lord, Ex 3:2, 20:1, stone tablets
- O Flower of Jesse, Is 11:1-3, flower
- O Key of David, Is 22:22, key
- O Radiant Dawn, Ps 19:6-7, sunrise
- O King of the Gentiles, Ps 2:7-8; Eph 2:14-20, crown
- O Emmanuel, Is 7:14; 33:22, chalice and host

Bringing alive this story of the Generations preceding the Birth of the Savior helps children and adults grasp the Mystery of the Coming of the Messiah as a tiny Child in a manger in Bethlehem, who, like us, had a "Family Tree."

113
Long-awaited Messiah

It would be a delight to read for ourselves and our children the entire book of Isaiah at least once during Advent. It emphasizes more than any other the great event of history—the Coming of the Messiah!

What we call the Book of Isaiah is considered, by Protestant and Catholic Biblical Scholars, to be three books. First Isaiah 1-39, called the Book of Judgment, was written sometime between 742-687 BCE and develops a spirit of threat and condemnation. Second Isaiah, Deutero-Isaiah, 40-54, called the Book of Consolation, was written between 550-540, before Cyrus of Persia let the Exiles return; it is a book of consolation and shared sorrow to the Exiles. Third Isaiah, Trito-Isaiah, 55-66, was written 538-510, after Cyrus proclaimed the return of Exiles; it focuses on visions.

Second Isaiah hearers are no longer inhabitants of Jerusalem but exiles in Babylon. Remember the sad Psalm, "How can I sing a song...?" Jerusalem has been destroyed and awaits re-construction. Babylon is no longer an ally, because she has destroyed Jerusalem and has deported the Israelites, especially those who are gifted and wealthy.

Just as it is with us, being swept off our feet by crisis and challenge and change sometimes teaches us a lot about life. The Israelites had to take on a new name, a new language, a new way of life, a new way of worship (without Temple and former religious practices), and they learned a new emphasis in theology—God is not only in Temple-Church, but in the hearts of humankind. The

Israelites took on a more personal responsibility, consciously chose monotheism over the many gods worshipped by those around them, shared in each other's' sufferings, and realized they were now living under a New Covenant.

Top that with the reality that their children had gotten accustomed to a new way of life and did not want to accept old traditions. Sound familiar? We do not even understand the language of texting, and our young people can no longer spell the English language! OMG. O My God.

The reading from Isaiah on Call, and the one from Thessalonians also on Call, asks us to comfort those in refugee camps, women and men who are trafficked by the greedy, the homeless in our own streets, people suffering from a flu epidemic and those engaged in their healing, relatives who suffer from addictions, incarcerated men and women who are away from their families, and the stray sheep that Jesus would have us gather into our communities.

Isaiah is about Hope—for the long-awaited Messiah!

114
The Whole World is Waiting for Love

The Whole World is Waiting for Love (song by Marianne Misetich SNJM) could be a title for readings of Advent. God asks us in Isaiah to "comfort, comfort My People." Mark invites us to "prepare the way of the Lord." And Peter assures us that all of our efforts will eventually bear fruit, as we "await a new heaven and a new earth." Reflecting on this, I say to myself, "God really loaded this season with reasons for celebration." Before December 25th, we celebrate December 6th Feast of St. Nicholas, and December 8th Feast of the Immaculate Conception!

Advent is indeed a season of "awaiting," but it is also a season of "acting"—of embracing the needs of others: comforting those who are suffering; seeking out food, clothing, toys, shelter, for the hungry and abused and homeless; preparing and strengthening hearts through prayer for the coming of the Son of God Who is the Self-Revelation of the God of Love; and asking God to let us know the gift of ourselves which might make the most difference to this "whole world waiting for love."

I heard a story the other day that moved me, and other hearers into the Advent Spirit. It goes this way:

> An eight-year-old boy asked his friends, who were coming to his birthday party, to bring gifts for poor kids instead of gifts for him. His friends' responses were so heartening to him that he decided to ask his Pastor if he could make an announcement from the pulpit, asking people to give toys and gifts for others instead of asking for Christmas gifts

for themselves. The Pastor hesitated, called the boy's home, and was assured by the boy's parents that it was his own idea and that they had not put him up to it. Because the boy had a speech impediment, he practiced and practiced in order to stand before the Congregation to make his request.

Maybe together, as members of our families and parish, we can be the hands and hearts and voices of God, helping to create a new heaven and new earth by the ways we comfort and love people in this section of the world into which we have been sent as disciples—despite our "speech impediments."

115
Always a Chance to Start Over

How magnanimous of the churches: to give us a chance to start over, every year! To continue hoping for the "More" of God in each year that unfolds. We pray the Advent prayer, "Come Lord Jesus, Come." Our Liturgical Year invites us to journey with Jesus the Christ through the realities of: birth at Bethlehem, life in Nazareth, suffering in the Garden, death at Golgotha, and Resurrection by the side of His Father. Advent is our Season of Hope, so desperately needed at this time in our history of: tsunamis, typhoons, volcanic eruptions, a nation where Congress agonizes over personal or party agendas versus what is best for all citizens.

When I was in Vietnam I met a youth of 17 who speaks Hope to my soul every time I look at the statue he carved for me from river roots. He is deaf, but determined to earn a living, and to teach other young people to be creative, entrepreneurial, and resourceful instead of begging. He collects roots of trees from rivers, dries them, carves beautiful statues of Jesus, Mary, Joseph; animals; figures that earn enough money to care for his ill father and 3 siblings. Our students flew back to the USA with T-Shirt-wrapped Holy Family and socks-filled Virgin Mary statues, and I sent Ho Phuong Hung An nearly $2,000. As the Catholic Relief Service cards say: Hope is Peace, Growth, and Opportunity!

Hope is one tough virtue to "pin down." The book I love, *Basic Verities*, written in French and English by Charles Peguy, refers to this theological virtue as "My darling little virtue Hope," great antidote to Worry. We talk, write, and pray about Faith and Charity; Hope seems to be the fragile virtue in the background. Yet, Paul's strong letter to the Romans paints a picture of Hope: "all creation is groaning in labor pains—in Hope, we are saved." One Biblical Translation reads, "all creation is waiting on tiptoe..."

Pope Benedict XVI picked this theme for his encyclical, "in Hope we were saved" (Rom 8:24). Hope helps us face the present, even if it is bleak and mysterious, and live each day sure of our Goal, as we pray, "Come, Lord Jesus, Come."

116
Advent: Season of Hope

Of the theological virtues, Faith, Hope, and Charity, it is Hope that opens up our whole person to the possibility of Believing and Loving. As a worrier "oldest kid" I reflected often on Charles Peguy's words in the book I previously mentioned, *God Speaks*: "Now I tell you, says God…without that one little budding of Hope, the whole of my Creation would be nothing but dead wood…Hope is the shoot, and the bud of the bloom of Eternity itself."

Theologically, Hope is the desire and search for a future good, difficult but not impossible to attain. Hope is opposed to both despair and presumption. In the Hebrew Bible (OT) Hope was important in preparing Israel for the Incarnation. By Jesus' Incarnation and Resurrection, humankind was "begotten again unto a Living Hope (1 Pet 1, 3). Hope can continue even when charity has been lost! And, sometimes recent elections, wars, human trafficking, out-sourcing, foreclosures, and other human heartbreaks and tragedies lead us to wonder if Charity has been lost in the Cosmos. Another Advent gives us a chance to remember that Hope does open the doors again to Charity and Faith.

LIVING IN JOYOUS HOPE

To live in Joyous Hope might be a possible summons to each of us. I recall the day I opened the door to a department store for a woman, smiled, and stepped back for her. She "chanted" over and over: "Thank you for smiling at me. Thank you for smiling at me. People don't smile at me!" Soon a group of about 12 people gathered around us—and yes, smiled. What if we smiled at everyone we meet, so they might see in our faces Joyous Hope? It's the "incarnation" of Emily Dickinson's poem, "Hope":

Hope is the thing with feathers,
That perches in the soul,
And sings the tune—without words,
And never stops at all.
And sweetest in the gale is heard;
And sore must be the storm,
That could abash the bird,
That kept so many warm.
I've heard it in the chilliest land,
And on the strangest sea;
Yet, never, in extremity,
It asked a crumb of me.

117
Jesus, Incarnate Word

John's Gospel begins: *"In the beginning was the Word, and the Word was with God, and the Word was God. He was in the beginning with God, and all things came to be, through Him."*

Before John, Proverbs 8:22 reflected: "The Lord begot me, the first born of His ways, the forerunner of His prodigies of long ago. From of old I was poured forth, at the first, before the earth." In theological language Christians hold that Jesus Christ as the Incarnate Word of God is God's supreme self-communication. We know this Jesus as a very real Person, as the God lying in a manger, the Healer walking streets of Nazareth, the Savior on the Cross who cried out to His Father, and the Glorious Resurrected Son who left us the Spirit. God in human skin!

Though Incarnation sounds like such an abstract Christian doctrine, the "wow" of the Incarnation as God's self-communication in this, that God is "en-fleshed" and by our sides at our wedding, at the birth of the first child, in challenges at work, in the doctor's office when we receive frightening diagnoses, during struggles to find prayer time, in all our consolations and crises. Most of our human events we Catholics sacramentalize. Judaism and Christianity are earthy Religions that lift together earth and heaven.

God actually brought the world into existence as receiver of God's self-communication. That is why we honor human existence from the moment life begins until we leave our heritage of wisdom to posterity. That is why we enjoy using our bodies to ski, dance, throw basketballs, and yell at hockey games. That is why we offer tender embraces to those whom we love. That is why we weep when children offer us hand-made Valentines or Christmas cards. That is why St. Irenaeus proclaimed: The Glory of God is the human fully alive!

That is why three Wise Persons from the East brought concrete "worldly" offerings. And that is why we celebrate the Birth of Christ with gifts and "I love you" words that we may put off the rest of the year. We are ourselves en-fleshed human beings in this real world, trying our best to say "yeses" to this Self-Communicating God.

118
Transforming the Ordinary

Jesus Son of God, Savior, The One who transformed the world, forever. The Heart of Christianity is transformation, of ourselves and our world, not flight from the ordinary. Jesus the Eternal Word became incarnate, took on human flesh like ours, and with it, all the human ordinariness of work, prayer, friends, misunderstandings, and tears of disappointment over Jerusalem. Like Him we are the children of Judaism: of Moses who made excuses when Yahweh invited him to do something but eventually became a great leader, of Sarah who laughed but became mother of nations. That Jesus, the Incarnate Son of God, the Messiah, the Savior of all humankind, was always a Jew with a Jewish Mother and foster Father.

Theologically His Mother Mary, an ordinary village girl who said "yes" to God, is called *Theotokos*, Greek for "God-bearer." She was mother of One Child, but in that capacity, mother of us all.

The faithful Joseph, father of a child somehow not fully his, coped with taxes, housing, re-location, and he still astounds us, in our world where lifelong commitments are difficult to make.

Ordinary people - homeless shepherds and Eastern travelers - in the Christmas narrative were messengers of God.

An older prophetess, Anna, was still praying in the temple many years after her husband's death; one would think she had nothing to anticipate, but she discovered new truths.

And ourselves? We transform the ordinary by: re-directing our latte or coke money to Oregon Food Bank until January; re-creating the "climate" in the family or workplace by replacing negative or loud speech with affirmations and soft tones; using a half hour of TV time for centering prayer, spiritual reading, or reflecting on the protests in the Prophets' words from God; taking a slice of time to serve at a homeless shelter or talk to people at McDonald Center; writing a Congressperson about a matter of injustice when we feel like griping to friends or relatives; "kything" our prayers to include the people of Egypt, Syria, and places of unrest; and continuing to stretch our world views to a global consciousness—a world that Jesus came to transform into a place of compassion, love, and WELCOME TO ALL

119
Dialectic between Religion and Spirituality

This "divergent" topic seems to fit our "global" consciousness: celebration of Mary Immaculate Patroness of the United States; visits of people like Bishop Remi DeRoo, one of the Vatican II living Bishops; Advent Season; and cosmos-shaking events in our world. This is the world to which our children and grandchildren are exposed, so their questions are religious, political, economic, humanitarian, scientific—and personal.

One of the heartaches I hear from parents of these children is: "They don't go to Church; and I so wish they would join me for Christmas Mass. They say they're committed to a spirituality, but want nothing to do with religion." This "spirituality" could arise from spiritual dabbling, putting together spiritual practices from Native Americans, Hindus, Buddhists, with no serious demands for *metanoia* (self-emptying, on-going conversion). But it may come from serious seekers who have found organized religion a hindrance to a deep desire for personal growth in union with the transcendent (God)—a sincere God-quest.

Let's look at "religion" from three levels: (1) the fundamental life stance of one who believes in the Transcendent, however named, and a realistic stand in face of Ultimate Reality, giving rise to reverent adoration and recognition of the need for divine help to live and serve; (2) a spiritual tradition, like Christianity or

Hinduism; (3) a religion or institutionalized formulation of a spiritual tradition, like Anglican Christianity or Reformed Judaism. Although "spirituality" was a Christian term, it is now used broadly; as this description by Peter VanNess: "...the embodied task of realizing one's truest self in the context of Reality apprehended as a cosmic totality. It is the quest for attaining an optimal relationship between what one truly is and everything that is; it is a quest that can be furthered by adopting appropriate spiritual practices and by participating in relevant communal rituals."

The "spirituality" of people who are traditionally Catholic remains religious in the first sense given above. They believe in God, in God's relationship with themselves and all beings, in union with a God that is life-enhancing, has an ethical dimension, and in the importance of spiritual practice and morality for union with God. It's worth a rich Advent discussion: for ourselves and our family members.

To be continued....

120
The Heart of Both Spirituality and Religion

To continue the dialectic between Spirituality and Religion. At its most basic, Religion is the fundamental life stance of the person who believes in God (the Transcendent, however named—Trinity, Yahweh, Adonai, Allah, the Absolute, Creator, the Holy One, Supreme Being, Uncaused Cause)—and assumes the posture of dependent human who needs to love and adore that God, and has a moral responsibility to treat one's neighbor with compassion and justice. Without this, Religions become shells. Our children and friends who claim an authentic Spirituality share this first sense with those who profess a Religion in all three senses: (1) the foregoing, (2) a Spiritual Tradition like Christianity, and (3) a denominational Religious Tradition like Catholic or Orthodox Christianity. That's one reason why the Mystics of West and East can make retreats together, understand each other, work for peace and justice side by side—like Thomas Merton and the Dalai Lama.

So, what's to understand about reasons people have moved away from Religion in the latter two senses? With interreligious experiences in a postmodern climate of globalization, they have become problematic for believers. First, denominational religions have been culturally, geographically, tribally, doctrinally, cultically, and even psychologically EXCLUSIVE. I recall my teen-age attempt to co-teach a Bible class with a friend, to fourth graders in a Methodist Church. The pastor stood in the doorway and said to me, "We do not encourage outsiders."

Secondly, and understandably, Religions hold to a set of beliefs, obligatory practices, and prohibitions. After exposure to a world of complexity and pluralism, even some fair-minded people question some beliefs, practices, and prohibitions as arbitrary or questionable or NOT APPLICABLE TO ALL persons everywhere in the world. Mature seekers are looking for, in their God-quests, spiritual breadth and depth, autonomy of conscience, and psychological maturity.

Finally, a third objection is CONFUSION about superiority or inferiority in one's ability to "get access to God." Vatican Council II, in the document on the Laity, wrote that Laity are made to share in the priestly, prophetic, and kingly office of Christ. It's not primarily the role of priest or sister or brother to be holy or to "do" the sacraments. All of us have a universal call to holiness. Living this call as a community, not simply alone, gives us gifts of accumulated wisdom and support to progress in the spiritual life, to be holy—together.

121
Godbwye

How many times a day do we Americans say: good-bye, good day, good evening, good afternoon, good luck, take care, see you, so long, farewell, cheerio, toodles, tata, take it easy, adieu, even, “Go, the Mass is ended”? Jesus said His “good-bye” at the Ascension and promised to send the Paraclete. We plan many farewell or good-bye events for presidents, civil servants, retirees, graduates, employees, friends, and relatives. We have touching ceremonies to honor our dead heroes. We plan a funeral to recall again the treasured moments of a person’s life.

Etymologies of words always fascinate me—in any language. Earlier forms of Good-bye in English came from such expressions as: God be wy you, god b’w’y, godbwye, god buy’ye, good-b’wy. Possibly “good” eventually replaced “God” as expressions like “good day” or “good luck” or “good night” or “good afternoon” became common. Shakespeare used “God be wy you.”

And so, it is time for me to say “Good-bye.” I am so very grateful for the years with which many of you have blessed me and loved me, while I participated in the Mission of a Catholic theologian to spread the Good News and endeavoring to make the enduring truths of Christianity relevant for this time in history.

My family members are becoming more and more frail. According to them, it is my “job” to make sure they all get into Heaven before I die. At present many are not Church-goers, though they are loving, ethical, spiritual people.

We "Rangers" are a bit of an "Irish clan" so our cousins are about as close to us as are our siblings. According to the "clan" of uncles, aunts, cousins, siblings, I am expected to pray for all of them, and their families and friends, and have my entire SNJM Congregation do likewise. Because my life has put me on the "active" side of "contemplation in action," I have had limited time to complete several books that sit like mosaic pieces on my computer.

Hence, I say with Shakespeare: "Godbwye."

About the Author

PERSONAL INFORMATION

Dr. Cecilia Ranger's lifelong commitment is that of educating and drawing out of people questions which will lead them to personal integration, finding a meaningful life path, discovering a spiritual home, and determining a vocation in life—thus, her commitment to education, theology, and to spiritual direction. Her passion is dialogue among the religious traditions, to bring together diverse positions on spirituality and ethics—in life situations, conversations, and in the workplace—as a means of helping to bring about world peace. So, it's been a rich life of interactions with God, people, and the beautiful world that we all try to preserve for the generations after us.

MINISTERIAL IMNFORMATION

Former Mt. Angel Seminary Professor & Spiritual Director;

Spiritual Director & Professor, St. Mary's Seminary and University, Baltimore, MD;

President of Oregon Sisters of the Holy Names;

Chair/Dean of Religion & Philosophy at Marylhurst University;

Board of Trustees Member, Marylhurst University;

Adjunct Professor at Marylhurst University, San Francisco Theological Seminary, Clark Community College, George Fox University;

Pastoral Assistant at the Madeleine Church, Portland, Oregon;

Facilitator of Workshops on Spiritual Life, Theology, or Scripture;

Consultant for Leadership Groups; Co-Minister at Marylhurst U;

Spiritual & Retreat Director for persons of many Faith traditions.

You May Wish to Read

Aquinas, Thomas - *Summa Theologica*

Breathnach, Sarah Ban - *The Simple Abundance Journal of Gratitude*

Burghardt, Walter SJ. - *Christ in Ten Thousand Places: Homilies Toward a New Millennium*

Cahill, Thomas - *How the Irish Saved Civilization*

Cain, Susan - Quiet: *The Power of Introverts in a World That Can't Stop Talking*

Carroll, James - Christ Actually: *Reimagining Faith in the Modern Age*

Chittister, Joan OSB - *The Art of Life*

Coleridge, Samuel Taylor - *The Complete Poems*

De Chardin, Teilhard - *The Divine Milieu*

Dersiewcz, William - *Don't Send Your Kid to the Ivy League Schools*

Dickinson, Emily - *The Complete Poems of Emily Dickinson*

Doherty, Jerry C - *A Celtic Model of Ministry, the Reawakening of Community Spirituality*

Edwards, Jonathan - *Sinners in the Hands of an Angry God*

Elizabeth Liebert SNJM - in *The Way of Discernment,*

Gandhi, Mahatma - *The Story of My Experiments with Truth*

Hopkins, Gerard Manley SJ - *The Major Works (Oxford World's Classics)*

Johnson, Elizabeth A. CSJ - *Truly Our Sister : A Theology of Mary in the Communion of Saints*

LaCugna, CatherineMowry - *God for Us*

Loyola, Ignatius - *Spiritual Exercises*

Moltmann, Jurgen - *The Spirit of Life*

Peguy, Charles - *Basic Verities*

Pope Benedict XVI - *In Hope We Are Saved*

Pope Francis - *Gospel of Joy*

Rahner, Karl SJ - *The Mystical Way in Everyday Life*

Ricoeur, Paul - *Time and Narrative*

Rosenberg, Marshall B. PhD. - *Nonviolent Communication*

Solle, Dorothee - *Choosing Life*

Vatican Council II - *Lumen Gentium (Dogmatic Constitution on the Church)*

Vatican Council II - *Unitatis Redintegration (Decree on Ecumenism)*

Vatican Council II - *Apostolicam Actuositatem (Decree, Apostolate of Lay People)*

Made in the USA
Middletown, DE
17 September 2018